Endless Perfect Circles

Lessons from the little-known world of ultradistance cycling

Ian Walker

World-record route
from North Cape to
Tarifa, 2019

North Cape

Oulu

Vyborg

St Petersberg

Suwalki

Plock

Hof

Strasbourg

Bayonne

Burgos

Merida

Seville

Tarifa

ISBN 978-1-83853-555-1 (print), 978-1-83853-554-4 (ebook).
First published July 2020.

For more information about the author, visit **drianwalker.com**

Introduction

Nobody talks about the ecstasy.

People who take part in sport spend a lot of time talking about what they do, but they never seem to discuss the most interesting part of it. We've all read, and heard, so many words on the pleasures of winning contests, of being crowned the top athlete of the moment. And perhaps there are people who can use these occasional and fleeting moments of triumph as motivation for the years of grind that are necessary to reach the top of their game. Good luck to them.

More astute sportspeople get closer to the truth when they say that what really matters isn't winning, but rather the love of the athletic process: the day-by-day focus on improvement, on watching the numbers get steadily better through deliberate and painstaking work, on controlling what you can control and letting the results fall however they will. These wiser souls say that victory is little more than a by-product of a perfectly executed training plan and race-day strategy. They note that the true goal is nothing more than performing to the best of your ability while under pressure.

But they still don't talk about the ecstasy.

They don't talk about the pleasure – the perfect, unalloyed *joy* – of running down a mountain trail and watching your own body dance over the rocks and roots as though controlled by a far better runner than you. All those hours of practice allow your legs to think for themselves, seeking out the ideal line, the perfect footfall, always several moves ahead of your sluggish mind. Your waking self is shocked when it sees your foot land exactly on the fragment of safe ground between two loose rocks, and all it can think is: *of course I stepped there! How could it have been otherwise?*

This thrill of controlled motion can also be found on a bicycle.

I pity you if you have never experienced it. If only I could make you feel the awe that can overwhelm you as your body and your bike begin to intertwine. I have gasped aloud in delight as I felt myself relax into the frame, my muscles and bones becoming inseparable components of the machine that thrills across the tarmac beneath me. There is a sensation of the divine as you realise that your legs could not, in any conceivable universe, be pushing in more perfectly timed circles than they are now.

This state of sublime connection – of *flow*, as it is known to psychologists – is only there for those who work for it. It is the athlete's great secret, the true reward for the hours of dedicated practice. It is only when all the focused repetition has turned the activity into second nature that your body can shake off your mind and perform its magic while you watch astonished, like a passenger on somebody else's journey.

And these moments are mercurial. They never come when you summon them – they appear at times of their own choosing. Often they last for mere seconds before the strings are cut and you fall back into the usual, mundane relationship with your body. When this happens, it is the same sense of bereavement that we feel upon waking from a dream with the realisation that we can never recapture the freedom and delight of a moment before. *I thought I could fly, but it wasn't real!* For that reason, when these moments of physical connectedness arise, you hold onto them like a butterfly in your fist.

And, on rare occasions, the instances of ecstasy last longer. I well recall the time when I was riding my bicycle alongside a Norwegian fjord at the end of a 4300-kilometre race from Italy to the northernmost tip of Europe. I won that race, but the greater reward was to be granted three whole hours of feeling unimaginably connected to the act of physical motion. As the still, dark waters slipped by on my right, a playground for the shadows of the clouds that skittered overhead, and as white reindeer grazed along the roadside to my left, I thrilled as I realised that the perfect state of being at one with the machine was not going away. Every motion of my legs was timed with picosecond precision, the power transferred seamlessly from my body to the road by the wheels that emerged beneath me like an offshoot of my own flesh. And that feeling lasted... and lasted... and I feel such gratitude for the experience.

That, perhaps more than anything else, is why I do sport. This feeling of connection is the ultimate reward for all the work – made all the sweeter for being meted out with maddening irregularity.

And, fickle as the experience is, I know that I would never find it at all if I didn't work so hard to look for it.

You have to do something difficult to get it.

What I did

I spent forty years believing I had no ability or interest in sport. Then I became a champion ultradistance athlete and broke the world record for the fastest bicycle ride across of Europe. This is the story of how that unlikely change came about, and what I learned along the way.

The book you are reading is necessarily many things. It is partly a travelogue, because my lessons came from crossing continents and thrashing myself to the ragged edge to do so. It is partly a memoir, because I cannot explain why and how I raced across those continents without telling you a little about myself. Finally, because I am a teacher and cannot help myself, this is also partly a textbook. I have distilled and shared what I have learned about undertaking extreme bicycle journeys so that you can take this knowledge in comfort. I talk about the practicalities of doing long self-propelled journeys. But more importantly, I explain what I have learned about the mental side of endurance, and how to keep yourself going when pushing yourself inevitably gets tough. These lessons from endurance sport translate surprisingly well to everyday life. That often gets tough too, and what we learn from enduring on a bicycle can teach us a lot about how to get through difficulties off the bike.

Part 1
Running

My relationship with sport

I blame football. Indeed, I blame it twice.

I blame football for why I spent most of my life believing I had no ability in sport. My school, like many bog-standard comprehensive schools in the 1980s, was staffed with bad teachers who were further beaten down by their disputes with the Thatcher government. We had a 70-minute period of team sport timetabled every week, but this almost always consisted of the games teachers handing us a football, pointing at the field and telling us to get on with it while they disappeared for a smoke.

The only exceptions I can remember to this diet of football were a single lesson in my third year of school when we didn't quite play rugby, a single bizarre lesson the following year when we didn't quite play American football, and one week each year where we carried a vast bag of cricket kit down to the field and spent 40 minutes donning the unfamiliar pads and setting up the wickets before realising we had run out of time without a single ball being bowled. We replaced the pads and stumps into their mildewed canvas bag, dragged them back up the hill, and put them away in the cupboard for another year.

All other weeks, for five years, it was football. But the thing is, in the UK, by the age of 11, you can already either play football or you can't. I couldn't. It just hadn't formed part of my childhood so far, and I couldn't do it. The sports teachers' laissez-faire approach meant they never gave us any coaching in how you played the game. And by that, I don't mean they failed to drill us in team tactics or formational play: I mean they didn't teach us the much more basic skill of how you used your foot to move the ball. It was assumed you already knew all this and the teachers' role was limited to – shall we be charitable? – giving us the space to develop uninterrupted. They contented themselves with being absent for fifty minutes and then reappearing to watch us go through the communal showers at the end of each lesson with an attentiveness we found unsettling even at the time.

All this meant that my formative experiences of sport involved standing in the rain, miserably watching other boys kicking a ball in the distance and regretting the hair mousse that we all slathered on our heads back then as it washed down into my eyes and mouth.

So in summary, I credit my school, and its lazy use of poorly supervised football, for decades of feeling that sport just meant being wet, bored and blinded by cheap petrochemicals.

I also blame football for my having no interest in watching sport.

I don't think people who enjoy football realise just how unlovely and threatening that sport can appear from the outside. This is true today, but it was particularly true back in the 1970s and 80s. When I contemplated my looming adulthood, as a youth growing up in east Lancashire, it largely felt as though the rest of my life would be spent in places of sudden and random violence – workplaces, pubs, football matches... all appeared to me as if they would be smoky, unwelcoming, hyper-masculine and, above all, dangerous. I was prepared to take limited risks with pubs, despite their violent and unpredictable appearance, because they seemed the only way to access beer and girls. But football – apparently even more violent and hyper-masculine than the pubs... well that could bog right off. And, as football was quite literally the only game in town in east Lancashire, all other sport was tarred with the same brush for me. School had shown me I could not do it, and nor did I want to watch other people do it if that involved a substantial risk of being pissed on or assaulted in the queue for a meat pie. Balls to sport and all who sail in her.

And so the years passed.

A single step on a journey can only ever feel small

My mid-30s rolled around. I lived a pretty sedentary life. I taught psychology and conducted research in a university – a career that does not place undue physical demands on a person. I occasionally dabbled in a bit of leisurely bicycle touring around the valleys of Wiltshire on a Saturday afternoon, but I travelled most places by motorcycle. My evenings were largely spent sitting around, drinking too much, watching television and not doing very much else. I was getting pretty fleshy and unhealthy. I was, in short, living much like most other people of my age.

Once a year, I would pull a rucksack on my back and go on a walking trip. With the exception of one Easter when I went over to Spain to walk an old pilgrimage route, I did this on the UK's National Trails. Wanting to learn more about possible routes, I joined an organisation called the Long Distance Walkers' Association, or LDWA. I became a member to access information about footpaths, but soon became aware that there was a lot more to the LDWA. In particular, I learned that their calendar pivots around a weekend in May each year, when they hold their annual hundred-mile walk.

My first response to seeing somebody mention a hundred-mile walk was for my eyes to skip back across the words, as if I assumed it was a typo and was trying to decipher the real meaning in the sentence. But eventually I had to concede that it was not a typo, this was real. People got together in large numbers once a year and walked a hundred miles. Wow. Good for them, I thought.

And then, over the following weeks, the notion started to eat away at me. In quiet moments I found myself wondering what it would feel like to walk that sort of distance. How would it be to stand on the start line, clutching a map and contemplating the enormity of the journey ahead? What would it be like to walk into the night and still be walking when the sun came up the next day – and then maybe even to do that again through a second night? People talked about the blisters, and the hallucinations. It sounded awful... yet fascinating. What would it be like to be able to tell people you have *done* that? To casually drop into conversation lines like 'Something I learned when I walked a hundred miles...'?

I found myself doing some research.

It turned out that the LDWA don't just let anybody turn up and try to walk one hundred miles at their events. You have to prove yourself by walking fifty or sixty miles in another event beforehand. So I signed up for a fifty-mile walk around Hertfordshire late in the summer of 2012. My feet exploded. I fell asleep across the footpath in the small hours of the night. But I eventually made it round, feeling broken and exhilarated in equal measure.

The next Spring, at the hundred-miler, I got blisters on my feet the like of which you cannot even comprehend. I swapped shoes to relieve the pressure, but this just created a new colony of even larger blisters on the few parts of my feet that were so far unscathed. These blisters stood almost a centimetre proud of my feet, and when I burst one at the half-way checkpoint, it unleashed a fountain of liquid that pulsed into the air for whole seconds, much to the delight of the walker sitting next to me. The last 20 miles of the event were walked at an unimaginably slow pace as I summoned all my resources to keep moving through the pain. When I hobbled into the school hall that held the fin-ish, I wept with relief and delight when the room applauded my entrance. I can still make myself cry today just thinking about it.

And then, my mission complete, I forgot all about walking and immediately went back to my old life.

A few months later, six weeks before my fortieth birthday, I got an email from my friend Rick with a link to a video of the Transvulcania race in the Canary Islands. This 73-kilo-metre run starts on a beach, climbs to the top of an enorm-ous volcano and then races back down to a beach on the other side of the island before jinking back inland, up a short and very steep climb, to the finish. The video looked incredible, with stunning scenery and crowds of excited athletes having the time of their lives. Rick's email said 'If you can walk 100 miles, I reckon we can do this'. The video looked so appealing there was only one possible reply: 'Fuck it, let's do it'.

I can be quite impetuous sometimes.

My reply to Rick was on the last day of September, which left me seven months to go from doing no running at all to running a mountainous ultramarathon at the start of May. Although several good books have been published recently on how to train for ultras, there were fewer resources back then. What I found instead was guidance on how to train for marathons. So I found a marathon that took place just be-fore Christmas and entered that, thinking it would focus my mind. Then I headed out for my first 5 k run. In three months – in violation of all the usual advice given to new runners – I went from doing no running to successfully running a marathon in a time that was not too embarrass-ing. The race was really tough, and I had plenty of occasion to wonder what I was doing to myself as I pounded along the course, but I successfully completed the marathon. I was light-headed and astonished as I ran the final stretch down Portsmouth seafront on jellied legs, talking out loud to myself as I passed the applauding well-wishers: 'I've done it! I've actually done it. I'm a *marathoner!*' I told myself.

And here's something I noted the following day: if I had set out only to run the marathon, the whole thing would have been far more difficult and daunting. But because the marathon was always just a step towards the ultramarathon, I found from the start that it was far less intimidating than it would otherwise have been. It was as though the marathon was a hill, appearing small and manageable because my gaze was fixed on the vast mountain that stood beyond it. How can something overwhelm you when it is only a step on the way to something bigger?

This leap into running saw a decade of sloth drop away from me, and with it went around 12 kilogrammes of body fat. As May approached, the remaining few months saw me step up my training even further. As I ran and explored, re-petition meant I got to know every footpath within 10 kilometres of my home with the deep familiarity of a woodsman: *here* is the beech root that protrudes higher than you expect and which has to be jumped; *here* is the patch of earth that becomes slippery whenever it rains. The training was hard, but enjoyable. I watched myself fall into the rhythm of being a regular runner, and started to feel ill at ease on days when I did not train. I entered a couple of local ultramarathons – 50 kilometres and 40 miles – as well as two 50-kilometre social runs organised by a group of runners I found on Facebook.

Looking back now, as I write this, I'm astonished at just how fast I progressed by throwing myself into running so profoundly. It is helpful that I have every run logged in Strava, a social media site where people share records of their runs and rides. If I had relied on memory to write this, I would never have got the details right. Was it really only six months after that very first 5 k run that I finished fifth in a 40-mile off-road race around the Pennines? How the hell did I do that? Again, I can only conclude that having the huge goal of Transvulcania looming on the horizon made everything else seem manageable in comparison.

It never always gets worse. It never always goes well

Transvulcania was as wonderful as I hoped it would be. Standing on the beach at the start line was as close to a religious crowd experience as I'll ever know. The sound system pumped out AC/DC and my chest vibrated with the noise and the excitement as a packed throng of two thousand excited runners bounced and surged in the pre-dawn darkness. There are sights I'll never forget from that race: the trail formed by hundreds of headlamps snaking up the zigzags of a switchback mountain trail in the darkness; dawn breaking over La Palma viewed from on high; the bruising 25-kilometre descent from the top of the volcano. I didn't eat enough and as a result I ran out of blood sugar and bonked badly on the final uphill slope. The led me to spend an hour lying helplessly in the gutter at the side of the road watching other competitors stride past as a huge shirtless Spanish man tried to coax me back to life. With his encouragement, and a sachet of energy gel borrowed from a passing runner, I eventually made it up onto my knees and from there back to my feet, whence I hobbled up the final slope to finish the race in the top half of the field. My mission complete, I ended the race by vomiting half-digested energy gel over the legs of an elderly Spanish woman who chose a bad moment to walk past.

In the following days, this finishing position in the top half of the entrants became a revelation to me. *I can't do sport*, I thought, the legacy of my school still strong in my mind. *How did I lie on the floor for an hour yet still beat more than a thousand other runners?* Slowly, over weeks, I began to realise that the belief I was physically inadequate, which I had carried around for years, had to be wrong. The only explanation for finishing in the top half of the field despite my lengthy lie-down had to be that I was actually fairly good at this sport – indeed, better than average. This was a profound shift in my self-concept, and one that I still struggle with after so many years of believing the opposite. Thanks a lot, school.

Transvulcania led to several more years of running, which was hugely rewarding. I learned that ultrarunners tend to be some of the nicest people around. I'd never encountered a community so friendly and welcoming. I joked that this was because running very long distances is the opposite of working in finance: it's really hard and you don't get any reward for doing it. Only people with great hearts are going to get involved in something like that.

More seriously, what bonded this community, and made it so welcoming, was the mutual respect afforded to practically everybody who was prepared to make the effort. It didn't matter how fast a person was: the main thing was that they were willing to have a go at these huge running challenges. It was interesting to see how the vast scale of these ultradistance races meant that every part of the pack looked at every other part of the pack with bemused disbelief. The slow runners marvelled at how fast the people at the front of the race were. But the people at the front, in turn, were astonished by how the runners at the back of the field had the fortitude to keep moving for perhaps twice as long.

Four months after Transvulcania I ran my first hundred-mile race and then, exactly three weeks later, I ran my second hundred-mile race. (This was not a wise decision. Don't do this.) From there I was hooked. Ultrarunning became a huge part of my life, and took me to some incredible places: I ran in the Alps, the USA and Nepal, as well as a lot more races in the UK.

When things went well, they went really well, and I found that I generally finished races in the top 10% of the field. Discovering that I was quite consistent in this was astonishing given my lingering self-doubt when it came to my physical ability.

Perhaps the highlight of my running career was the 100-mile Ultra Tour du Mont Blanc (UTMB) – the de facto world championship of mountain running on a beautiful but gruelling Alpine circuit with over 10,000 metres of climbing. Crossing a high mountain pass into Italy after eleven hours of running and watching the sun rise over a cloud inversion far below my feet remains one of the most beautiful sights I have ever experienced. The race unfolded almost exactly to plan, and I was able to achieve my goal of not just finishing in a reasonable time, but also of running in strongly at the finish instead of limping to the line in the usual way of amateur 100-mile finishers. It was the best example to date of sorting out the pacing and self-control that are essential to long-distance success.

But that triumph in the Alps sat alongside my various defeats, and I had to learn quickly how to deal with big unexpected setbacks. I suffered badly from the effects of altitude and got timed out after sixty miles on the Leadville 100 in Colorado. I didn't eat enough on the Verbier-St Bernard race and crawled ashamedly onto a rescue bus on top of the St Bernard pass (having just walked into Italy from Switzerland without my passport, which I'm not sure is entirely legal). I contracted trench foot after 150 miles of a 185-mile race along the Welsh-English border. The trench foot was astonishingly painful, like having a shoe full of broken glass, and I was forced to drop out. The saving grace was hearing non-running friends say things like 'You only had 35 miles left to run!' and then laughing as I realised it was the first time they had put 'only' and '35 miles' together like that. It was nice to shift people's perspectives.

Catastrophic foot infections notwithstanding, it was during these years of running that I learned to be at peace with suffering. I suspect you cannot do well at endurance sport unless you achieve this. For example, until you have been there, you cannot begin to grasp the reality of being 85 miles into a 100-mile race for the first time. By that point in the run, your legs no longer bend, every muscle in your torso aches from holding yourself upright, your feet scream, and the 15 miles of the course ahead of you might as well be an infinity. You are no longer in charge of your destiny, you are merely managing your decline as best you can. All your world is pain. Summoning all your resources, you push yourself out of your seat, leave the warmth of the aid station and attempt to start running again. The result is a pathetic hobble and you give a hollow laugh as you re-member the easy pace you were putting down at the start of the race. It seems so long ago that it might as well have been an ancestor who was running. You shiver in the cold night air; you know you should stop and pull an extra layer of clothing from your pack but you cannot summon the will to do it. You have tunnel vision, unable to see anything other than the path ahead. At the same time, another part of your mind is screaming at you to stop this insanity, and re-minding you that this is entirely voluntary. *You can just quit! Go back to the aid station and hand in your number. Who's going to care if you do?*

So how do you keep going when you are so desperate to stop?

A big part of it is having been there before.

Exposing yourself to a long difficult experience is like sail-ing along a series of waves. You go up then down then up again, over and over. But the series of waves is not steady and regular. The difference between the peaks and the troughs gets larger and larger as time goes on. In the early stages of a race, the waves are mere ripples, their dips and rises inconsequential – you perhaps notice that the running feels slightly harder for a while and then, some time later, it feels easier again. But as the event continues to unfold, the peaks start to get higher and the troughs lower. After twenty hours of running, the low points see you collapsed in a shrub gazing into an existential void and the highs feel like you've been injecting mega-heroin.

Once you've ridden that roller coaster a few times, you gain enough experience to trust the process. When the bad times start to come... it's fine, because you were expecting them. *Hello, Pain,* you think. *I was wondering when you'd show up.* Later, at the really low points, when you're desperate to quit, you can make use of your knowledge that it will get better. You learn that your task when you start to feel low is not to try and improve your situation – your job is simply to keep yourself moving, knowing that, sooner or later, matters will settle down of their own accord.

While there is no real substitute for having been through this roller coaster experience and seeing for yourself how bad feelings always eventually fade and disappear, you can shortcut the learning process a little by listening to the wisdom of more experienced athletes. There are certain phrases that get repeated over and over in the ultradistance athletics world which, while simple, capture a great deal of important truth. And this truth goes far beyond sport – these are truths about everyday life as well. You only get one attempt at life, but endurance sport is the nearest you'll find to having a practice.

So what are these wise sayings from the experienced ultradistance athletes?

"It never always gets worse." Let's be honest: sometimes, when times are hard, the next thing that happens is that it gets even harder. One setback follows another, and then there's another setback on top of that. But it never *always* gets worse. If you can just wait it out – if you can just keep going, no matter how slow or messy you look as you do so – eventually things will turn around. That's true in everyday life as well, but ultrarunning is a great place to experience it in miniature, at a time of your own choosing.

"Constant forward progress." Every step forward, no matter how small, is useful. It's just true. The speed you move forward will go up and down – but as long as you're pointing in the right direction and doing *something* then that's always useful.

"It's just one foot in front of the other." This sounds like such a simplistic, banal thing to say. But trust me, when you're in a mess, those words are like the wisdom of Solomon. I was at the half-way point on the Leadville 100 race – an event that starts at 10,200 feet (3100 metres) and goes up from there. I lived at 45 metres above sea level, which was not good pre-paration for racing two miles up in the sky. Hammered by the effects of altitude, I'd limped over Hope Pass, stopping from time to time to have a hefty vomit by the edge of the trail. Drained of all energy, I was now slumped in a chair cradling a small plastic cup of noodle soup which I couldn't make myself swallow. I wanted to quit, and said as much to one of the aid station volunteers. I was going too slow. I was never going to finish the race in time. 'No, you can still do this,' he said. 'I was in the same state as you when I ran UTMB. All you have to remember is that it's just one foot in front of the other. Keep doing that and you'll get there.' And this was solid advice. Getting back to the start of the route, fifty miles away, was too much to contemplate. Even climb-ing back over Hope Pass to the Twin Lakes aid station ten miles away seemed impossible. But one foot in front of an-other... I could do that. And then do it again. Reducing an enormous task down to a simple, concrete action genuinely helped. This approach has got me through a lot of tough times since then.

"If you can't change your circumstances, change how you feel about them." My health psychology colleagues who work on chronic pain have a lot to say about this. There are some medical conditions where, sorry, but you're going to be in pain for a long time. Maybe for the rest of your life. That's really shit, but there's only one healthy approach when faced with that reality: accept it. If something in your life absolutely cannot change, then wishing it away is a waste of effort. It's probably also a way of making yourself pay more attention to the problem, not less. Although this might be easier said than done, the best thing you can do is accept reality and move on. This might mean distracting yourself,

it might mean making peace with the reality, it might mean making changes to your self-identity, it might mean raising it with other people at every opportunity... whatever it takes in your case. But when circumstances definitely can't change, don't waste time wishing it were otherwise.

All this and much more I learned by putting myself into the crucibles of suffering that are ultrarunning races. These events provide a test-bed to stress yourself, learn to cope, and bounce back stronger. Even when I didn't manage to finish a race, I found it rewarding – although, to be sure, it might be a few days or weeks after the event before I fully appreciated this and saw what I had learned.

And then, at the end of that great summer centred on running UTMB, and just as I was really starting to feel like I was getting the hang of distance running, I gave it all up overnight and started riding a bike instead.

Part 2
The Transcontinental Cycle Race

The Transcontinental Cycle Race captured my imagination and wouldn't let go.

One way to describe the Transcontinental Race is to quote its founder, Mike Hall: "At the sharp end it is a beautifully hard bicycle race, simple in design but complex in execution. Factors of self reliance, logistics, navigation and judgement burden racers' minds as well as their physiques. The strongest excel and redefine what we think possible, while many experienced riders target only a finish." Those are words to manage your expectations about how easy something is going to be.

More specifically, the Transcontinental sees several hundred riders gather at a point in Europe – Geraardsbergen in Belgium, in the year I did it – and ride to a distant point on the other side of the continent as quickly as possible. In 2017, the fifth time the race had run, our goal was Meteora in Greece – a distance of just under 4000 kilometres for most people. If I sound vague about the length of the event, it is because riders in the Transcontinental are free to choose almost any route they please, as long as they hit four mountain-top checkpoints along the way. This makes the race so much more than just a simple test of who is the strongest. The rider with the best legs won't win unless they are also good at route planning. Each person has to make their own decision about how comfortable they feel taking quicker, busier roads or sticking to safer, but slower, back lanes. Almost everybody who has ridden the Transcontinental has an anecdote about a road that looked perfect on the map but which turned out in reality to be a broken dirt track that vanished in the night.

But even strength and planning are not enough. Success in the Transcontinental is above all determined by how you handle a clock that never stops. This is not a stage race, but a nonstop push. If you pause to rest or eat, the clock continues to tick. If you need to make a repair or fix a puncture, other riders might get ahead of you as you work. This unceasing timing throws up a hundred decisions about strategy, tactics and equipment. To take just one example, the risk of punctures forces you to ask whether you will fit tough tyres, which are less likely to get damaged but which roll more slowly, or instead fit lighter, faster tyres, which carry an increased risk of being damaged. Once you've decided on that trade-off, you have to decide if you will carry a spare tyre, or save the weight and accept a small risk of getting stranded should one of your tyres get torn irreparably.

The tactics of sleep become critical. How little do you think you can get away with? And how different will that be after ten days of hard physical work – something you might never have experienced before? Will you ride straight through the first night to try to get some kilometres in the bank, or will you put yourself onto a sensible overnight sleeping schedule from the start even if this means other riders pulling away from you as you snooze? Each evening, as the sun goes down, you have to decide whether to press on to the next town – perhaps several hours away – and hope to find a cheap hotel, or to bivouac by the roadside but risk being woken by rain or traffic in the night. Perhaps you do something more imaginative and shift your rhythm around completely, riding through the night and sleeping in the afternoon to avoid the draining summer heat. But this in turn forces you to consider whether you have lights that are good enough for nocturnal travel and whether you are able to find enough portable food at the right time of day to get you through the hours of darkness... The permutations can soon become overwhelming.

Finally, and above all, success in such a race requires you to possess such personal qualities as willpower and toughness. Strength, planning and tactics all count for nothing if you are not able to dig down within yourself and find the ability to *just keep moving* through whatever setbacks emerge, day after day after day. Because there *will* be setbacks. There always are. Your ability to race the big miles is determined as much as anything by how you handle them when they appear.

As soon as I had the idea to enter the Transcontinental, after stumbling across an article about it, I hardly slept for the next two nights. I lay in bed picturing what it might be like to undertake something so *big*. I'd run in a race that lasted around three days – which was epic as far as running races go – but how would it be to put my life on hold and hand myself over entirely to an athletic endeavour that went on for two weeks or more? What would it be like to ride alone through distant and intimidating corners of Europe like Serbia and Macedonia – places I only knew from harrowing news reports in the 90s – in the middle of the night? To be entirely self-reliant in the face of enormous adversity? Learning the answers to those questions wasn't just something I wanted to do, it was something I was *compelled* to do. I pulled out of all my planned running races for the coming year, threw aside the years of training and development, and became a cyclist instead.

Since then I've learned to pay attention to ideas that grab me like this. When an idea takes root so easily and so firmly, it's probably the right one.

A happy coincidence around this time was that I moved from where I was living just outside Bath into my girlfriend's house on the edge of Bristol. For the last year, I had been running to and from work at the University of Bath most days, and this had been a great way to get training miles into my legs as part of my daily routine. Indeed, I was even briefly featured in *Running* magazine when they did a feature on commuting. This had all been a useful arrange-

ment when my commute was around 11 kilometres each
way, but was no longer an option now I was living at least a
72-kilometre round-trip from work. The shift to bicycle racing fit perfectly with this change of home, and I was able
once again to use my regular commute as part of my training. Most mornings I would ride through Bristol city centre
and out to Bath along the lumpy and overcrowded Bristol-
Bath Railway Path before coming back the same way in the
evening. My body responded by becoming more muscular:
my weight rose by 3 kilogrammes and stayed steadily at this
new level.

To get some experience with longer rides, I began to go
out on Audax UK events. The term 'audax' refers to slightly
different styles of cycling around the world, but in the UK
it's a form of long-distance self-paced riding.[1] People get together at a pre-arranged time – usually slightly too early in
the morning – and then ride a fixed route of 200 kilometres
or more, each going at their own speed. Riders need to get
round the course before a relatively generous cut-off time –
typically 14 hours for a 200-kilometre ride – but audax is
otherwise firmly non-competitive. No record is kept of the
finishing order; riders either finished before the cut-off or
they didn't. As such, nobody is racing and it is far more
common to find yourself having a chat with other riders
than it is trying to drop them on the climbs.

After a few months I realised that, although I had ridden
over 200 kilometres on three or four occasions, I was still
nowhere near the sorts of distances that would be required
if I were to make a serious attempt at the Transcontinental.
Moreover, not only would the race require me to go much
further than I had ridden so far, I'd also need to get up the
next day and do it all over again. I had not yet ridden two
long days back to back, and so resolved to see what that
would be like, at least once. I decided I would find some-

1 In some parts of the world, this would instead be called *randoneur-
ring*, and the term audax would refer instead to long-distance
guided group rides. It gets needlessly complicated quite quickly.

where 300 kilometres from home and ride there and back within a weekend.

Scanning a map revealed that Sheffield is almost exactly 300 kilometres from Bristol. That was the sort of journey that most people would think twice about driving, which was a daunting realisation, but I went to my favourite route-planning website and got to work.

The ride up the country was tough, and I had to dig into my *just keep moving* experience more than once, but I was elated as I eventually dropped down a hill into Sheffield and watched my odometer tick over from 299.9 to 300.0. Wow – three hundred kilometres, under my own steam. I felt a warm glow as I checked into a little hotel that I knew from some earlier work trips, walked stiffly down the road to in-hale a big curry, then crashed out for a few hours of deep, restful sleep.

The next day, just as dawn was breaking through the frigid air, I was back on the road, puffing big clouds of vapour and trying to loosen my calves on a long climb out of the city. As I reached the top of this first big hill and emerged onto open moorland dotted with twisted black trees, the sun broke out behind me and spread soft light across the rolling grasslands. The sun then made a complete traverse of the sky and had disappeared behind the opposite horizon by the time I made it home that evening, broken but thrilled. Knowing I was capable of riding two big days back to back raised my confidence considerably.

Spring rolled into Summer, and I took every opportunity to slip in extra training miles. The build-up to the Transcontinental peaked with a brutal audax ride called the Pendle 600. Six hundred kilometres around the north of England taking in every 25% and 33% slope that the sadistic organiser could find. The total ascent was over 10,000 metres. At a petrol station, late in the first afternoon, I met a cyclist called Richard Coomer and we elected to ride together through the night as the route criss-crossed high passes in the lonely darkness of the north Pennines. Richard would later became a valued companion on several future long rides, but that day we went our separate ways at the 400-kilometre point, where the ride organiser had arranged a village hall in Cumbria where we could rest. I fell asleep for two hours on top of half a congealed pizza, while Richard took a shorter break and got back on the road while I still snored. We bumped into each other again near the end of the route, and were among the first riders back to the starting point the next day. I counted myself ready to race.

Transcontinental Cycle Race number 5

I had to get moving.

I was enjoying the sunshine, slumped in a chair outside a German cafe with a large half-finished glass of Coke in my hand and a big contented smile plastered across my face. But I had to get moving. I couldn't stay here.

To my side, the Rhine ran lazy and slow between a series of steep cliffs. Above, perched impossibly on the hilltops, fairytale castles looked down on the cargo barges that rippled the waters beneath. It was a jarring combination of the magnificent and the mundane. But I couldn't remain here and enjoy the contrast any longer. The clock was ticking.

This was the first full day of the Transcontinental Cycle Race. The previous evening we riders had gathered in Geraardsbergen where, once unleashed, we crashed like a wave up the cobbled flank of the Kapelmuur. The route out of the town was lined by cheering spectators, their faces sinister and mysterious in the flickering light of the burning torches they held as they roared their support. It had been exhilarating to be in that dense swarm of cyclists, each of us facing the same way, each riding too hard towards a common goal as if with one mind. Snatches of shouted conversation flashed past in half a dozen languages, all the time enveloped by the din of the onlookers.

Then, abruptly, the crowds had fallen behind and I was out in the stillness of the Belgian night. My hands rested comfortably on the bars and my feet glided around in endless perfect circles, the excitement of the event pushing my pace slightly higher than the measured and conservative effort I had planned. Finally underway after all the waiting, my doubts fell away as I settled into the familiar act of cycling. My body knew what it had to do. *It's like riding a bike*, I thought to myself, and laughed. Red tail-lights, some blinking and some steady, streamed away into the darkness ahead of me as the cool air rushed over my smiling face. I glanced back and saw a matching stream of white headlamps behind. For a few minutes I rode alone, and then fell into a pack of riders, only to lose them again when I turned left at a junction while they all pressed on ahead. Each of us had already worked out our own path, kept carefully secret from all other riders, and there was no reason to think I would see any of these people again. As I rolled through a silent suburb I plucked a can of Red Bull from my jersey pocket and drank it without even pausing in my pedal-stroke.

And so that first magical night passed. Giddy with disbelief at the unfamiliar experience of being in such an epic race, I slipped unsuspected through the sleeping town of Waterloo and then crouched low on the aerobars as I pushed down long, straight and deserted roads towards the Netherlands. Dawn broke, bright and filled with promise, as I crossed the border near Maastricht. It seemed as if hardly any time had passed before I was in Germany, where I dropped onto this smooth path by the Rhine – not the most direct route between Geraardsbergen and the first checkpoint in southern Germany but, I hoped, flatter and faster than the more obvious route through the hills of the Ardennes. Through it all, I rested on my handlebars and pedalled, the smile still upon my face, until I reached this cafe and decided I could spare five minutes for a big cold drink.

But that time had passed. I had to get moving. This was a race, after all. I would have to reach the end before I would be freed from the awful tyranny of the clock.

oOo

I went into the Transcontinental Cycle Race with no real expectations. As the phrase has it, I was there to complete, not compete. If asked, I might have said I hoped to get to the end of the course in time for the finishers' party, but the Transcontinental is so big and tough that I would have been happy simply to finish and have that tale to tell. These expectations were sensible: in most years the Transcontinental sees around one-third of the riders finish in time for the party; one third finish, but after the party had ended; and one third drop out of the race somewhere along the way (or 'scratch', as it is known among riders).

So it was a surprise to roll into the first checkpoint in Germany, after about one-and-a-half days' riding and a brief roadside sleep, to learn I was in 24th place. There were around 250 riders at the start in Geraardsbergen, so somehow, without doing anything particularly special, I was inside the top 10% of the field already. This will sound like false modesty to you now, but I honestly did not expect this – this was my first bicycle race and I was only there to see if I was capable of finishing. I did not know I had the slightest chance of being competitive: this felt a world apart from the running that I knew and I had only started cycling properly a few months earlier. At the pre-race briefing, as I had surveyed all the gleaming bicycles and calf-muscles, it seemed clear I was going to be outclassed by pretty much everybody else there. So learning that I was in a reasonable position at this point was as surprising as it was gratifying. Fellow rider Josh Cunningham had rolled into the opulent hotel that hosted the checkpoint at the same time as me. I turned to him as we ate breakfast amongst the murmured conversations and tinkling china. 'Well,' I said, 'I guess I'd better start taking this race seriously.'

It was time to go to Italy. Checkpoint 2 was at the base of Monte Grappa, on the far side of the Alps. The temperature almost at once became oppressive, and over the course of the next day my thermometer climbed from 11 degrees all the way up to 40. None of us in the race realised it at the time, but this was the start of a Europe-wide heatwave so long and deadly that it became known as The Lucifer.

I pushed through this heat to cross the southern half of Germany and then into Austria – a 300-kilometre day. As the night began to form off to my right, the Alps appeared on the horizon and inched towards me. I slept for a few hours in a small hotel in Lermoos and then headed back out before the sun rose. I had the roads to myself so early in the morning. The smooth Austrian tarmac slipped under my wheels as the moon dramatically backlit the peaks on the horizon. Wrapped in the cool pre-dawn air and surrounded by the hushed majesty of the Alps, that first hour was transcendental as I headed through a series of sleeping villages to reach the main road and the Fernpass.

At that time of day the traffic was light and I was soon over the pass and eating a three-course breakfast in the service area on the far side as the sun came up. I felt great. I was riding the biggest ultracycling race in the world, I was performing better than I had expected, and I was feeling great. Also, my omelette was marvellous. You can't ask for more than that. The smile I wore in Germany was still on my face. Thank goodness I had taken the plunge and exposed myself this way despite all the fear I had felt at the thought of such a huge undertaking. Imagine having missed this experience because I hadn't dared try.

Ride angry

Along the River Inn to Innsbruck, then a hard turn south to climb over the Brenner Pass. I smashed the climb because I had misremembered its altitude and so it proved to be far easier than I was expecting. Almost before I knew it, I was at the top of the pass thinking 'Was that it? That was *easy*.' Like how my first marathon had felt manageable because I was focused on the ultra that was coming next, anticipating a bigger climb on the Brenner made the reality seem trivial. It's all about expectation.

Then it was a long, hot push down a series of valleys as I moved across northern Italy. Motivated by my placing at Checkpoint 1, I got low on the aerobars and really put in some hard hours, pushing harder than I had for the last couple of days. I was rewarded by passing several other contestants. I was also briefly confused by seeing a scattered handful of riders coming in the opposite direction, each with a race number attached to their bike and each, like us, loaded with bikepacking kit. What was this other race we were overlapping? No time to think about that too much, though – I continued to press hard along a series of well-paved cycle tracks running through orchards, stopping regularly to fill my bottles from the water fountains that stood at convenient intervals. I overtook several more Transcontinental riders and started to congratulate myself. I couldn't wait to get to Checkpoint 2 and see how far up the rankings I had risen from these two days of hard racing effort.

And then it all went wrong. I did a thousand-metre Category 1 climb over the Passo della Fricca which, I soon discovered, was completely unnecessary. I even pushed my bike for a couple of kilometres on the old rocky footpath that flanked the mountain at the top of the climb, because riding through tunnels was forbidden by the race rules. It turned out that, while I went on this adventure, every other rider had taken a lovely flat cycle track around the base of the mountain that I had completely failed to notice during my route planning. I only discovered my mistake when I was in a small town on the other side of the pass, eating a takeaway pizza in the humid darkness that had followed the sunset. Each rider in the race carried a satellite tracker that updated their position on a website every few minutes, meaning people back home could follow the race – and meaning also that we riders could keep track of one another. This was how I discovered my route-planning error on that close, sweaty night in Italy. As I chewed my pizza I refreshed the race tracker on my phone and swore when I saw what a setback I had undergone. The pizza was disappointing too. I threw it into a bin and remounted the bike.

Three hours of angry pedalling later, I pulled into Checkpoint 2 to find that I was back in exactly the same position I had been at Checkpoint 1. Thanks to my bad route planning, two days of intense riding in blistering heat had gained me precisely nothing in the race. Shit. I had to press on. I had to get that time back.

The Transcontinental generally allows riders a free choice of route, but each year there are a few short mandatory sections, mostly near the checkpoints. Immediately from Checkpoint 2, we were forced to climb the full height of Monte Grappa – a mighty Alpine ascent so intimidating it earns an Hors Categorie classification: it is 'beyond categorisation', or 'off the scale' for cycle races. Monte Grappa climbs 1500 metres up an average gradient of more than 8% on a road that threads through a series of tight hairpins to what was once a wartime killing field. It was also entirely the wrong direction for people trying to get from Checkpoint 2 to Checkpoint 3, included by the organisers purely to maintain the race's reputation for toughness.

Other riders were bedding down on the floor in quiet corners of the hotel that housed the checkpoint, waiting to tackle the climb in the morning. Still stinging from all the places my routing error had lost me, I set out to get over the mountain in the darkness while this lot slept. The climb took two hours and forty-three minutes. I fell over twice after pausing and then trying to do hill-starts on the steep slope in total darkness. The climb was so overwhelming that I had to fall back on all my running experience, breaking down the enormity of the undertaking and keeping myself firmly in the moment. *Just keep turning the pedals and you'll get there eventually*, I thought. I focused only on the next switchback. There was nothing beyond it – to reach that next bend was all that mattered. And when I eventually got there, all that mattered was to reach the next. Like some serial philanderer, I pursued each corner as if it were all that mattered in my life, only to abandon it and lunge for the next as soon as I had what I wanted.

Eventually reaching the monument at the summit, slightly bloodied and very weary, I found a rider whom I had last seen near the first checkpoint. I later discovered this was world-champion time-trialist Stuart 'Hippy' Birnie, but then, in the darkness, all I knew was that he was some guy with very deep wheels and an Australian accent. For a moment, we both gazed across the startlingly clear lights of the valley far below us. It was like the twinkling view from an aeroplane at night. Then, scenting a chance to drop a competitor behind me, I left Hippy and bounced down a broken track towards lower ground, at one point memorably swerving two badgers who leapt out into my path. But my competitive urge was fighting with fatigue, and half-way down the mountain I was overcome with a sudden and irresistible need to sleep. It came upon me so suddenly: one moment I was weaving down a broken road in the darkness, the next I was hit with a deep certainty that I had to stop immediately. I pulled over and looked for a spot where I could unfurl my bivvy bag, but at once a pack of feral dogs scented me and began to chase, barking furiously as they ran towards me through the darkness. I clipped back into the pedals and bounced further down the track, fighting the urge to close my eyes. It was only some time after three o'clock in the morning that I was finally able to bed down in a picnic site and grab a few hours' troubled sleep. At one

point I was dimly aware of Hippy's brakes squealing as he
rode past me, nudging me back a place in the rankings.

Big city, little speed

Sleep is amazing.

This thought looped around my mind as I crossed the
baked brown plains of northern Italy under the withering
sun and then rode into Slovenia. I had slept on the ground
for perhaps three hours, but this was all it took to act like
hitting a reset switch. Now, on my fourth day of riding, I
was back at a level of effort that I could not have imagined
at the end of the previous night. The restorative power of
even a brief nap was something I experienced over and
over through the Transcontinental. The phenomenon still
fascinates me today.

I passed through a town called Ajdovščina and then, as the
road climbed up into the hills, I really started to fall for
Slovenia. Green, idyllic, cheap and full of friendly people
who speak good English – what's not to like? As evening approached I stopped for a pizza at a restaurant near Vrhnika
and listened to a group of women on a neighbouring table
sing together as I ate.

Big cities are the enemy of fast cycling, and I first started
to realise just how bad they are for racing when I crossed
Ljubljana. It was a hot sticky night and the city, while trim
and attractive, had an air of overheated summer madness
hanging over it. People spilled out of bars; young men
drove too fast and aggressively up the boulevards. I was
stopped over and over by traffic lights, and watched my average speed plummet. Earlier that evening, as I was eating, I
had arranged a hotel in a small town a couple of hours past
the capital. But all the Ljubljana delay threw me off schedule. I was still in the city and had only around 265 kilometres under my belt for the day when I got an email from

my hotel saying their reception closed at 2200 and when was I due to arrive? I realised there was no chance I could get there in time. I cancelled the booking – reluctantly for-feiting the price of the room – and found an alternative hotel a few streets away. A warm welcome from the friendly manager. A large glass of cold beer that almost had me weeping with joy. A hot shower. Sleep. Sleep.

The next morning I was frustrated with my lack of pro-gress. I had only managed 267 kilometres the previous day despite having flat roads almost the whole way. Today it was time to toughen up. I bashed across the rest of Slovenia with my head down and soon reached Hungary. After Slov-enia, Hungary's countryside felt poor and rustic, its villages filled with unsmiling people sitting on the edges of potholed roads while drinking from hefty beer bottles. I pushed into the night, resolving to ride until I was too tired to continue. As the sun set, the cornfields that lined the road filled with the roar of a million crickets. The noise came from every direction at once, louder than I could have ima-gined. The throbbing wall of sound amidst the stifling hu-midity was almost overwhelming that first night, but as the race went on I started to look forward to the humid evening chorus as my sign that the heat of the day was finally over and I could pick up the pace as I rode alone into the cooler air of the night.

Eventually, in the small hours of the morning, I tried to sleep in a bus shelter on the outskirts of a town near Győr, but was driven away by the incessant barking of some dog driven insane by its life locked in a back yard. If the dog was loud enough to disturb the sleep of an exhausted TCR rider, what must it have been like to live near that house? I crammed my air mattress back into my saddlebag and headed further up the road. I eventually fell asleep under a shrub in a park until I was woken far too soon by two early morning runners crunching past my bed. I had managed 362 kilometres, though – that was better.

You can eat well, or you can eat quickly, but you can't do both

It is easy to get the idea that nutrition is everything in sport. Companies compete to sell perfectly balanced foods and supplements; books, magazines and websites are filled with information about the right combination of macronutrients for every phase of training and racing. Amateurs take cues from the professionals, and nowhere is there greater professionalism than in the top tier of cycle racing. The big grand-tour teams travel the world with full-time nutritionists and chefs, controlling every gramme of food that enters their riders' bodies to ensure optimum performance at all times. Carbohydrate and protein levels are adjusted on a meal-by-meal basis to respond to that day's training load and anticipate the physical demands of the next day.

This level of control in the professional peloton has filtered into public awareness. The comment I have heard more than any other from non-cyclists is something like 'I guess you must pay a lot of attention to nutrition when you're racing.'

Nothing could be further from the truth. In these unsupported races it is possible to eat well and it is possible to ride fast. I don't believe it is possible to do both.

Let's do the maths. Let's say you're riding in a 4000-kilometre race and let's say you're able to move at an average of 25 kilometres per hour (this is slightly faster than most people can ride long distances, but it makes the calculations easy). Let's also say you need 7 hours of downtime each evening to clean yourself and your kit, eat dinner, and sleep. This leaves 17 hours for all the day's activities – riding, bike maintenance, rest, buying and eating food… Now let's say that each day you stop for lunch at a cafe or diner (45 minutes) rather than grabbing cold food from a roadside petrol station, quickly gobbling as much as you can and then and eating the rest of your meal on the bike (15 minutes). Each day, that extra half hour to eat a hot lunch is putting you half an hour's riding, or 12.5 kilometres, behind where you would have been had you done the smash-and-grab at a petrol station. After 14 days, your lunches have put you 175 kilometres behind where you might have been. By foregoing those hot meals, you could finish the race almost half a day earlier. That is a big difference.

And that's just one meal each day. Let's go further. Let's say your desire for comfort means you not only have a hot lunch, but also stop for coffee in the morning (an extra 20 minutes over just grabbing and going) and stop for a pizza once every second day (an extra 45 minutes each time). After 14 days riding, you're now 423 kilometres behind where you would have been – that's well over a full day wasted just through wanting a bit of hot food. The other competitors are gone home by the time you finish.

I fully realise, if you do not race long distances, that this might all sound ridiculous. But I have learned to think this way as I tried, over a period of years, to ride faster for longer. You're never going to get much faster by trying to improve an already fit body; but dealing with all the time spent stationary during a long ride offers huge, and relatively easy, gains. As we will see, I became more and more strict about saving time this way as my racing progressed.

This brings us to the other side of the equation: by being disciplined and efficient you are now eating quickly, but you are no longer eating well. When the desire to save time means you are grabbing your meals from petrol stations and convenience stores, a typical day of ultracycling becomes fuelled almost exclusively by what my girlfriend dismissively calls 'brown food' – chocolate, pastries, potato snacks, muffins... anything fast, easy to cram into a jersey pocket and, above all, full of calories.

One convenience food, above all, has achieved almost talismanic status in the European endurance cycling world: the 7 Days croissant. Widely available from petrol stations all over eastern and southern Europe, these have as much in common with true French croissants as a teddy bear does to a Grizzly. Cheap, readily available, indestructible and packed with energy, 7 Days croissants have a level of convenience that tips the balance just enough for riders to endure their artificial flavour and alarming smell. The distinctive waft of sugary air that is released when the packet is opened is something I suspect I will still experience when all other senses have long abandoned me.

The wheels begin to come off

It was the sixth day of the ride, and Slovakia greeted me with a puncture. I rolled into the country on a bridge across the Danube from Hungary and instantly hit a big pothole that burst my front tyre with a snakebite flat. I pulled over onto a grassy area and put in a new inner tube, but then found it would not inflate. Suspecting that my pump might be faulty, I dug out my spare pump – but this was no different. I unhooked the tyre again to find this new inner tube also had holes in it. I replaced it with yet another, but could not inflate this either. What was going on? These were brand new tubes, fresh from their packets. I tried to patch the tubes, but struggled to get a good seal. This was ridiculous – I had dealt with scores of punctures in the past without trouble. What was happening now? I pulled out my phone and found a bike shop nearby, where I was able to get some new tubes. This was a relief, and I was glad I had been within a short walk of a shop, but the whole thing lost me over an hour. I couldn't stop thinking how much more serious this would have been had I been somewhere more isolated.

Three hundred kilometres ahead of me was a pass in the Low Tatra mountains – the last real obstacle before the mandatory climb up to Checkpoint 3 further north in the High Tatras. I pushed as quickly as I could across Slovakia, my head down, stopping a couple of times for meals and once more to repair another puncture. My first couple of hours' riding that morning had involved a whole load of stress and extra kilometres when Hungary's bizarre and arbitrary use of No Cycling signs had forced me to re-route near the edge of Győr. Now, in Slovakia, I somehow took a wrong turn and had to backtrack several kilometres. Then I almost rode onto a motorway by mistake. The day felt like one setback after another and I started to feel out of control. I felt I was waiting for something to go wrong from which I could not recover.

In the end, of course, it was not all setbacks. I should have known this and felt less anxiety. I had forgotten that essential lesson of long-distance athletics: it never always gets worse.

Something that came to mind that day was how one of the best things about unsupported ultradistance racing is that there is more than one way to be good at it. You can be a good ultradistance rider simply by being fast. But you can also be good by being a smart route-planner, or through being efficient during your rides and wasting as little time as possible off the bike. Each of these skills can compensate for the others, so it is possible to be fast overall, even if you are not a terribly strong rider, by being great at these other essentials.

Another key skill for a good ultradistance rider is being a problem-solver.

My problem-solving skills were called upon that day when my shorts began to chafe my crotch in the most unacceptable way. I don't want to get too graphic here, but the salt of my sweat and the seams of the shorts had combined to produce a kind of cheese-grater effect right on the parts of the body where you don't want that sort of thing. There was no way I could go further like this. I stopped on a quiet roadside to have a think...

Five minutes later, I was riding through Slovakia in a tiny pair of running shorts that I had brought as evening wear. But as these were unpadded, I had lashed my cycle shorts inside-out onto the top of the saddle so I could still enjoy their comfort without any of the chafing. Genius.

This kind of roadside improvisation illustrates another reason why I choose to put myself through lengthy and difficult challenges. A long race – or even just a long training ride – provides one difficulty after another: a tough climb, a mechanical problem, a dip in energy or motivation... Each of these is its own challenge, nested within the bigger challenge of the event I have undertaken. Each is an opportunity to push myself, and so get to know myself better. Each adversity tests me in a different way so that, by the end of the event, various facets of my character have been proven. In this way, I achieve a deeper self-knowledge and confidence from knowing I have prevailed repeatedly, on a broad range of trials. I carry these little victories with me, and I use them. On a difficult day at work, I might think *I can run a hundred miles*, or *I can cycle across a continent*, and at once my mood brightens, my shoulders move back and my self-confidence returns.

And if there is pleasure to be gained from overcoming a physical challenge, like conquering a difficult climb, how much sweeter to overcome a challenge of the spirit? There is no satisfaction like taking part in an event that initially frightened you but which later revealed you were capable of more than you thought. Or to sit slumped by the roadside, exhausted and overwhelmed, and somehow to find the strength within yourself to keep moving. This is why I make the choice to put myself in these difficult positions. To overcome a mountain is wonderful, but to overcome the mountains inside your mind is far greater.

I have never entered a race that did not, in some way, frighten me. Of course, the nature of the fear changed with the scale of the event. If I ran a 10-kilometre running race, the worry was only whether I might be a lot slower than I'd hoped. But when I stepped up to ultradistance racing, and especially when I moved into the extremes that come with ultracycling, I found whole new realms of fear to overcome.

No matter how skilled or experienced you are, there is always a strong probability you will not finish an ultradistance race. Too much is outside your control: weather, the roads, dogs and, above all, motorists. The true challenge, then, is not trying to win, or even trying to ride fast; the real challenge is one of character, of how you respond to adversity when it inevitably arises. Even in a race where you do not finish, victory is still truly yours if you are able to say, without reservation, *I did all that could be done; I could not have given more.*

The Tatry

Night arrived. Amidst the humid darkness and the throbbing noise of crickets I pushed into the Tatra mountains and climbed straight up to 1200 metres altitude. On the descent down the other side I noted how easy night riding had become. At first, riding in the dark had felt intimidating, but with exposure I had grown comfortable with it. Indeed, I was probably at the point where being comfortable tipped over into being complacent. Descending at over 50 kph on poor roads with my headlamp on its lowest setting to preserve battery life, I realised that the murky pool of light that shone ahead of me was manifestly not up to the job and so scrubbed off a little speed before I crashed in one of the potholes scattered so bountifully around this part of Slovakia. Equally pressing, I realised I did not have enough food for the night and that I was starting to feel weak. I tried a hotel but found it closed. Eventually, after 315 kilometres, I hit Highway 18 where, hungry and fatigued, I fell asleep on the floor of a bus shelter. I was woken every few minutes by heavy trucks whooshing by, but was stuck in the Catch-22 situation of being too tired to move to another place where I could get enough sleep to stop feeling too tired to move.

Eventually, at first light, I gave up on sleep. Thankfully, dawn always brings a fresh energy that cannot be found at four o'clock. I crammed my kit back into my saddlebag and began slowly to roll up the road where, to my relief, I found a village shop that was open surprisingly early. I sat outside and gorged myself on yoghurt, fruit and doughnuts.

Checkpoint 3 lay just up the road – in every sense of the word 'up'. Although only 6.6 kilometres long, the road to the hotel climbed the entire way with an average gradient of 10% – far steeper in places. Worst of all, the road was extremely narrow along its entire length. This meant there was no option to zig-zag from side to side and thereby smooth out the steepest sections. It was relentless. I met Josh Cunningham again at the bottom of the climb and we ascended together, bemoaning our lot and wishing we had lower gears. A professional cyclist in his youth, Josh later commented that this was one of the hardest climbs he could remember.[2]

Finally, eventually, the slope ended and there was the hotel that held Checkpoint 3. Round-the-world rider Juliana Buhring was helping run things, and nodded approvingly at my saddle-padding solution. More importantly, I learned that I was now up to sixteenth place in the race. This was amazing news. I said how surprised I was to have climbed up the field like this given all my punctures, pizzas and general faffing around. One of the checkpoint staff replied with what proved to be a very wise statement: 'A big part of these races is just keeping moving'. I was delighted to have jumped so far forward in the race. If it was true that keeping going was half the battle, and I had gone from 24th place to 16th place between the last two checkpoints... could I possibly be in the top ten riders at the finish? This immedi-

---

2 Now I've mentioned him twice, I should point out that Josh Cunningham is also an award-winning travel writer. If you're new to adventure cycling or long-distance bikepacking and want some guidance, I would definitely recommend his book *Escape by Bike*, which is both informative and beautiful.

ately became my ambition for the Transcontinental, and there was a lot of race left in which to achieve it. What a story that would be for a novice rider in their first race! I left Josh, who was slumped in a chair looking exhausted, and headed back down the slope and pushed back towards Hungary.

oOo

The following day I had my sights set on the Romanian border. I had the roads to myself as I rolled silently through the crisp pale sunlight of the early morning, watching birds flap over the wheat and cornfields. Once or twice a deer glanced up in the distance, alerted by my motion, and glared at me warily until I was gone. The pedals turned easily, and as they did I found myself slipping into a deep and true sense of awe at what I was achieving: the previous night I had crawled into a remote Hungarian hotel feeling tired and broken, and yet here I was, riding fast again, eating up the kilometres on a stunning day. *My body is amazing*, I thought. *I can do anything.* My eyes brimmed with tears of wonder and gratitude as I realised that here I was, doing things I would never have imagined myself capable of.

Of course, endurance sport always has its ups and down. And so, after experiencing such a high, it was only natural that a couple of hours later I crashed hard when my front wheel slipped off the sharp lip at the edge of some Romanian tarmac and I was thrown sprawling across the road. Luckily there were no motorists around at the time, but I was left with a series of painful, oozing grazes down my left arm and leg that covered my clothes, and later my camping mattress, in sticky blood. Years later, I've still not managed to get the blood off that mattress.

Food fixes everything

The Lucifer heatwave continued to smother the continent. I crossed Romania, beaten down by its heat and the appalling driving standards of the locals.

Riding a bike when it is 46 degrees Celsius is awful. It is not quite so bad when you are moving – it is surprising how much the flow of air over your body masks the worst of the heat – but the moment you pause, the full weight of the day lands upon you again, all the more shocking after a period of not noticing it. You come to loathe traffic lights for the pain they inflict. Perhaps the most dispiriting effect of these temperatures is that, within minutes of filling your bottles, your water rises to a temperature that is quite literally the same as bath-water. Drinking water that is hotter than your own body provides no refreshment at all, and nor does pouring it over yourself. I am from the north of England. These conditions are not something I am built for.

Eventually, the heat began to enrage nature itself. Late that ninth morning, 120 kilometres after waking up in a field, I looked up from the handlebars and saw the Carpathian mountains appear on the horizon. Towering above them, dwarfing the peaks, were stormclouds that rose until they disappeared from sight. It was like riding towards an apocalyptic black wall of infinite height and width. I felt miniscule, like an ant crawling towards the edge of the world across a dusty brown plain. I fished out my rain jacket as the first drops started to fall, and within moments was being stung by the weight of the downpour. I took shelter in a roadside cafe where I found fellow rider Tim Maundrell, who had taken an unorthodox route through the edge of Ukraine to get to the Carpathians but who would still go on to finish the race in 13th place. Together we sipped coffee and watched an ocean fall outside the window. It felt as though neither of us was in a hurry to leave our sanctuary, and not just because of the pounding rain – we knew what lay ahead.

The Transfăgărășan Highway was forced defiantly over a 2000-metre mountain pass by President Ceaușescu, showing all of his usual disregard for practicality and human life. It climbs up to a ridge that looks as though it should not be crossable, rising up a steep valley in an arresting series of bends and curves. Seen from above, the twisting, curling road resembles a rope flung across the landscape by a giant. Nobody even remembers how many soldiers died to build this marvel. As one of Europe's most dramatic stretches of tarmac, the Transcontinental race manual had said that it was not a matter of *if* the race would one day take its riders over the Transfăgărășan, but *when*. Our year was to be the one.

I learned that day just how much energy is required to ascend a long mountain climb. It took over two and a half hours to reach the highest point of the Transfăgărășan and I entirely underestimated how much food I needed to power that sort of effort. *After all, it's only climbing up a hill*, I thought, not appreciating that the difference between hills and mountains is more complicated than that. It was as though I still couldn't quite comprehend of any climb lasting more than an hour. In my defence, they don't where I come from. The longest climb within a day's ride of my home takes little more than 20 minutes.

I started out too hard and did not eat enough, so was bonking badly by the time I reached the final race checkpoint, part-way down the other side of the pass. The checkpoint was in another hotel, so I ordered two meals from the menu to try and fix my blood-sugar deficit. But I was in another Catch-22 situation: I was too weak to stomach the food I needed to stop me feeling weak. I pushed the plates away with their contents mostly uneaten and enquired about a room for the night – it was still early evening, but I felt that a few hours' sleep and an early start the next day might sort me out. But there was no room at the inn. Reluctantly, I remounted my bike and made slow, wobbly progress down the wooded valley until I found another hotel where I could get a room, but no food.

This all meant that the next morning, as I headed down the road on the south side of the mountains, I still had nothing in the tank. The route should have been one to lift the heart – a wide gorge lined with towering pines, cut through by a road that hugged the edge of a still, black lake – but I was past caring about scenery. I was so weak that, after two hours on a road that essentially ran downhill all the way, I had covered only 40 kilometres. Eventually, I found a hotel at the far end of the lake and bribed the receptionist to let me attack the breakfast buffet. He palmed my Euros and pointed me towards the dining room where I slumped at a table and called my girlfriend, Louise. 'I just don't have anything left,' I babbled. 'I'm only doing 20 kilometres an hour even though I'm riding down a mountain – I can hardly turn the pedals. And there are signs everywhere warning about bears! How am I supposed to outrun a bear like this?!' Her response was entirely correct: 'Eat. Just eat. Stay there for however long it takes and eat.'

I ate everything. Later that morning, I was not only back to normal but managed to clinch a top-10 performance on a long Strava segment along the Olt river.

This recovery proves that my only problem that day was lack of food. But, critically, the *experience* of not having enough energy was not the feeling that I needed to eat, it was the feeling that I was hopelessly out of my depth. Looking back now, in a more rational state, I can probably explain this...

Self-perception theory tells us that feeling an emotion is not a straightforward chain of events that always unfolds the same way. The emotion we feel in a given moment depends as much as anything on the label we attach to the feelings we are experiencing. So, for example, churning in the belly before a big event might be experienced as nervousness or excitement, depending on how you decide to label it to yourself. Clearly, one of these is a much more positive interpretation than the other.

In other words, we don't simply feel our emotions. Rather, a lot of the time, we are effectively watching ourselves and working out what we are feeling from the clues we observe. There in Romania, finding myself weak and ineffectual, I made a bad judgement about what this meant. Rather than reaching the right explanation for my state, which was that I had just not eaten enough for all the riding I was doing, I made an *internal attribution*: I decided that all the problems I was suffering came from who I was, rather than my circumstances. I became convinced that I lacked the character, training and skills for the ride I had undertaken. I started to think I was an idiot for ever believing I could undertake this race. I doubted myself. But food – and a good talking-to from Louise – can fix everything. It should be obvious you can't run an engine without fuel but the irony is that, the moment your energy supplies get low, the last thing you can do is remember this simple fact or deal with it properly. And, if you are anything like me, you might start explaining away the feelings that arise with a totally maladaptive interpretation.

Those days in the Făgăraș taught me how important it is to anticipate these situations, and to be prepared and disciplined enough to get food into me before it is needed when hard riding lies ahead. Failure to fuel leads to failure to believe. Never again do I want to stare into that particular abyss.

Pffft

Towards the end of my tenth day of riding, I passed through the Romanian city of Craiova without giving it a second thought. It was just another concrete impediment, as far as I was concerned. Dusty Romanian cities were just background to me by now. Fifteen kilometres later I was cresting the top of a hill on the DN56 road when I heard the sudden and dispiriting *pffft* of a puncture from my back wheel. What should have been a simple roadside repair became a race-destroying disaster. As the sun set ahead of me, I spent the best part of two hours fitting one inner tube after another and failing to get any inflated. Holes appeared in all of them, and I could not get these holes to patch up. A series of further frustrations began to pile up on top of this. The road was busy with noisy traffic, so that I had to wait for minutes at a time for occasional breaks when I could listen for where the air was escaping from the tubes. My pump then stopped connecting onto the valves properly, making my attempts to get air into the wheels fiddly as well as futile.

These punctures are still a mystery to this day. I know I nicked one tube with a tyre lever as I installed it, but I have no idea where all the rest of the holes came from. The tubes were mostly fresh from their packets; there was definitely nothing poking through the tyre, and no sharp spots on the wheel rim. I checked these with meticulous care at least a million times as I tried to get my tyre inflated. But every tube I fitted somehow turned into a colander as soon as I attempted to blow it up. None of the patches would stick properly, not helped by their glue struggling with the heat, humidity and dust. Eventually, slowly and reluctantly, I realised I was all out of tricks. I was forced to accept that I wasn't going to fix this.

There, on that dusty Romanian roadside, my dreams of a top-ten finish died.

It was fully dark by the time I slipped cleat covers onto my shoes and began the long trudge back towards Craiova, pushing the bike and phoning Louise to tell her what had happened. I clopped slowly for seven kilometres to a town called Podari, where I found a young man working in a cafe who spoke German. He helped me find a taxi that could carry a bike, and this took me the rest of the way back to the city. I slunk into a hotel and discovered that no bike shops would be open until 1000 the following day. Being forced to stop for so long was agonising.

The next morning found me camped outside Top Sport Bike, ready to pounce on the owner as soon as he arrived. I bought a fresh batch of inner tubes, and I watched jealously as he inflated one of them for me in two seconds using his compressed-air hose. I re-mounted, ready to cover the fifteen kilometres out of Craiova for the second time, but before setting off I took a moment to send out a message on Twitter. The finish line lay 855 kilometres away, through five countries. Stinging from all the lost hours, I decided I was going to ride the entire rest of the race non-stop. Such a crazy undertaking needed a suitably vainglorious name. I pulled out my phone and sent out a message on Twitter:

> **Right, I've finally got inner tubes but have lost a huge amount of time in the race. It's time for Operation Kickass.**

Operation Kickass

Eight-hundred and fifty-five kilometres, in one big push. Let's do this! I rode out of Romania, across the northwestern tip of Bulgaria on some truly shocking roads, and then into Serbia. Here I started to bump into other racers for the first time in days. I found German long-distance expert Michael Wacker riding with Melissa Pritchard, who would go on to be the fastest woman in the race that year. The three of us rode together for a short while, shooting the breeze and comparing notes about our adventures, until I slowly pulled away along a long, quiet road amidst the pale brown fields.

> **Operation Kickass sitrep: 200k and feeling okay. Serbia**

Then I found Swede Daniel Johansson standing by the side of the road sifting through one of his bags. I pulled over and we chatted for a few minutes. As I remounted and prepared to leave, I looked at my map and said, 'Hey look, it's only a short distance to Niš. There's a McDonalds in Niš.' Daniel's face lit up with a wide beam. '*Fuck yeah!*' he yelled. 'I haven't had proper food in three days.'

> **Operation Kickass sitrep. Nearly 300k. Slowed pace as Serbian roads are ropey in the dark. But feeling good. Onwards!**

I had just made a scary 10-kilometre U-turn on the A1 main road near Grdelice when I dropped off the tarmac onto a dirt track and found myself alongside Stuart "Hippy" Birnie once again. We caught up with each other's news briefly before my front wheel hit a big pothole and punctured. Hippy rode away as I pulled the wheel out of the forks. I got this puncture repaired pretty quickly, but it was a foretaste of what was to come as I went into the most frustrating night of my life.

The dirt road – already barely visible on my map – headed through the middle of a vast and confusing construction site where a new motorway was being built down the valley. In the darkness, with the ground churned and smashed by heavy vehicles, the true path at once became impossible to see. The surface of the road was indistinguishable from all the other dirt and spoil amidst the tyre tracks. I was forced to backtrack over and over as promising routes proved to be false, moving slowly over the broken surface and slithering in patches of mud and soft sand.

Part of the problem was that I could see nothing of my surroundings other than the little circle lit by my headlamp. In the daylight I would at least be able to see my surroundings and aim for a landmark, but at night I had no way to know where I was in relation to the other features in the valley. In a flash of inspiration I pulled up Google Maps on my phone and activated satellite view to see where I was standing relative to the real road, but the imagery in this area was far too crude and grainy to be useful.[3] Eventually I found what I thought was the right path and followed the track as it climbed uphill, only to find myself at the edge of a half-constructed motorway bridge surrounded on all sides by a fifty-metre drop to the ground below. And there, as I turned around atop a towering concrete platform that invited me to fall to a messy death, I heard a familiar sound in the darkness: *pffft.*

For the next two-and-a-half hours it was that dusty Romanian roadside all over again: one tube after another failing to inflate, one patch after another failing to stick. Except this time it was 3 o'clock in the morning and I was tired and dirty and hours away from the nearest town. One of my tyre levers snapped – hardly surprising, given I had used it to take my tyres off and on a billion times. On my knees, surrounded by the artefacts of my ineffectual repairs, I just wanted to cry. I dropped my hands into the soil and released a roar of rage and frustration into the darkness. Never, ever, have I wanted more for somebody just to come and make it all go away. If it had been possible to press a button and make it stop I would have done it. Had some-

---

3 Checking again, as I wrote this a couple of years later, I saw that Google's imagery in this area has now been updated. Looking today, I can see every detail of the the new motorway that curves sinuously down the valley. Damn its gleaming carriageways and all who use it.

body appeared in a helicopter offering rescue, I would have thrown my bike down in the dirt and dropped out of the race without a second thought.

(That moment, kneeling in Serbian mud and unable to move forward, has become a touchstone for my life. Since then, any time I have found myself feeling frustration or despair, I have always managed to pull myself out of it by asking myself 'Is this as bad as that night on the construction site in Serbia?' The answer, so far, has always been no, and this has been a very successful method for giving myself a sense of perspective. What a wonderful reminder of how these extreme sporting events provide a test-bed for suffering, a place to prove yourself and come away stronger than before.)

It took all my willpower not just to lie down and sleep in the dirt, but eventually I managed to get a repair patch to hold. I almost couldn't believe it when the tyre started to inflate. By that point I had been through the motions of mounting the tyre and connecting the pump so often that I had given up expecting anything to happen. But, wondrously, the tyre inflated and I was able to move again, hardly daring to breathe in case this somehow ruptured the patch. And then I managed to find the right track and get out of the construction site. I grinned with delight that I had overcome this whole string of challenges, one after another. I was so thrilled to have got myself moving again that I almost didn't care when I got chased by a pair of dogs and crashed my bike trying to escape them. Almost.

oOo

The next day saw me pass through the rest of Serbia. A backstreet tyre mechanic in a small village mended my inner tubes with heavy-duty patches, a pneumatic press, and glue so strong that it made the hairs in my nose shrivel and die. There was no way those patches were ever coming loose. He even waved away my offer of money once the work was complete. What a guy.

> Serbian tyre guy mended two tubes, booted my tyre and then refused payment. I LOVE him. Operation Kickass not dead yet

Tucked away in the Balkans and further isolated by war, Serbia had spent a long time cut off from the rest of Europe and as a result is its own fascinating world. Rather than the global mega-brands that make the rest of the continent so homogeneous, I found local varieties of everything, often with badly chosen English names. The ubiquitous Magnum ice cream couldn't be found in Serbia, but was replaced with the 'Macho'. I saw a shop selling a perfume called 'Economic Eau de Parfum' then roared with laughter after passing a restaurant called simply *Alas*. The temperature rose to 46 degrees as I climbed to the Macedonian border and demanded water from the guard who checked my passport.

> Operation Kickass sitrep. 455 km done, 397 km to the finish. Last night I hit new lows but that's past now. It's sweltering. #TCRNo5

Macedonia saw yet another mighty blunder, although at least this time I was not the only person to make it. Every map of Macedonia shows a nice big road – the R1312 – over the central mountains on the way to Prilep. Unfortunately, the R1312 is nothing more than a cruel cartographical fiction. The road is, in reality, a rocky goat-track that rises to over 1000 metres elevation. I climbed it in the depths of night, forced to push and carry my bike almost the entire way. It took hours. The rocks and sand destroyed my cleat covers, then my cleats, and then my shoes, and for the remainder of the race I could no longer clip into my pedals and had to make do with resting my feet on top of them. After many hours of bad-tempered pushing I found Daniel Johannson sleeping by the side of the track; a little while later I lay down myself and snatched three hours of troubled sleep amidst the scrubby bushes and coarse grass at the foot of a rocky outcrop.

And so it was a weary Ian who was sitting outside a petrol station the next morning when Melissa Pritchard rolled along. She was all smiles after a good sleep and an easy ride along some lovely smooth highway. She took a photo of me from below, emphasizing my chewed-up shoes. I later learned that a whole bunch of us fell for this R1312 trap. One French rider ran out of water during the long climb and got so thirsty that he spent half an hour on his knees licking a wet slick of moisture from the ground before walking around the next bend and discovering that the source of this wet slick was a bountiful natural spring that bubbled through the rocks at the side of the path. So I guess my experience wasn't quite as bad as his. But for me, yet another night of huge time-eating setbacks was a mighty blow to Operation Kickass and morale was in the toilet. *I just have to keep moving*, I told myself. *It never always gets worse.* But at times it was hard to believe this as I pictured all the other competitors who had passed me over the previous two nights.

oOo

The heat continued to sear the world as I crossed the border into Greece and turned to head southeast. The landscape here in northern Greece was extraordinary. Up on a plateau, and largely empty, the country had an epic sense of scale that verged on feeling eerie. It was impossible to judge the true size of anything. I rode past a power station that seemed like a toy amidst this vast, featureless landscape. This was not how I pictured Greece.

Here in the final country, I at last started to scent the finish line which had, until then, seemed too distant even to contemplate. The kilometres slipped beneath my wheels as I pushed hard through the astonishing heat, stopping only when the need for water forced me. Eventually, after ten hours of hard riding, I reached the final slope. This was it – after this climb it was downhill all the way to the finish. I resolved to hit the ascent with my last gramme of strength and leave everything I had out on the course. I emptied out one of my two water bottles to save weight and fired up the hill, little realising that the climb would take 47 minutes and leave me desperate for the water I had so rashly thrown. It was worth it though – I managed to get the fourth-fastest Strava time on that hill and then, as the sun set, I swooped down the other side of the pass, the astonishing hilltop monasteries of Meteora flashing by as I rolled into the town. I cruised down the main street, past bustling bars and restaurants, in a dizzy state of disbelief. I felt disconnected amidst the normality of the town; people went about their evenings as though some extraordinary feat of athletic endeavour were not taking place in their midst. The lights and noise were overwhelming to me after the stillness of the vast Greek interior. A couple of other TCR riders spotted me from outside a cafe and cheered my passage. I barely glanced over: at the end of this road was the hotel where the race would end. I swung off the road, deeply engrained habit causing my right hand automatically to click down two gears as I slowed...

It was a deeply anticlimactic finish to a life-changing ride over thousands of kilometres. There was no hype, no cheering, no cameras. There was not even anything to mark the location of the finish line. But in the circumstances, in this old-fashioned race where amateurs thrashed themselves to the ragged edge for no more reward than the recognition of their peers, this seemed entirely appropriate. I leaned my bike against a wall and walked up a few steps to where the race organisers and some of the previous finishers were sitting quietly around a table. Somebody handed me a cold can of beer. There were handshakes and quiet congratulations. I spotted the race winner, James Hayden, who had finished his ride in an astonishing time of just over 9 days. I shook his hand with a heartfelt 'Chapeau'. *I doff my hat*: the highest praise one cyclist can give to another.

I sat down, my ride complete.

After all my travails, after all that suffering, the heat, the crashes and the saddle sores, I had finished in 27th place out of around 250 riders. It had taken 12 days, 23 hours and 4 minutes.

oOo

A short while later, I sat slumped in my chair by the finish-line, sipping from another can of beer. I had been to a nearby shop, and the can in my hand had five siblings – one empty and crushed on the table, four more sitting in a plastic bag on the floor next to my chair. I was hoping to hand one to the next rider when they arrived which, according to the tracker, would not be long. I wanted to see whether their look of relief at being told the race was over would match mine.

It was dark, and the other finishers and race organisers were still sat around in twos and threes outside the front of the hotel, talking quietly in the warm night. As I savoured the crisp beer I was drinking and enjoyed the unaccus-

tomed pleasure of having no urgent need to move, a dangerous thought started to form in my mind. As I looked
back at the ride I had just completed – the heat, the punctures, the bivvys, the roads, the pizzas – I found myself fixing on a clear and startling realisation:
I could have done that faster.

Some lessons from the Transcontinental Cycle Race

Looking back on my effort in the Transcontinental, as I
write this, I am struck by how I was both accomplished and
naive. There were aspects of the ride that went really well,
given that I wasn't even riding a bike a few months earlier.
Enough time has passed that I am now largely happy with
my finishing position, all things considered. I am especially
pleased with how I was rising steadily in the placings until
those grim nights of suffering across Romania, Serbia and
Macedonia.

But at the same time, looking back with more experience,
I am frustrated at all the mistakes I made. Writing this section of this book forced me to reflect on my Transcontinental ride in more depth than at any time since I did it, and
there is a sense in which I now want to grab my past self
and shake him. 'Why didn't you take that obviously better
road, you idiot?' I want to shout. 'It's right there on the map,
parallel to the shitty strip of potholes you decided to ride
down! And while we're at it, what were you thinking when
you took that stupid pump you bought off eBay? I don't
care if it worked when you tested it in the shed! Why would
you take something that hasn't been tried again and again in
the field?'

There are some lessons I took from this race that were
quite specific to me, and might not be all that useful to
other riders. For example, I felt my daily distances were too
erratic. Even if we ignore Operation Kickass, I did days ran-

ging from 224 kilometres up to 566 kilometres. That, I felt afterwards, came from inventing my race strategy as I went along. I decided I would be happier next time if I had a more consistent plan for how I would ride. I was also annoyed at how often I had let myself get into a deficit with eating. Those bonks in Slovakia and Romania shouldn't have happened, and I resolved to be a lot more disciplined about this in the future.

There were also a lot of lessons I learned from that first big race that were more practical. In the interests of trying to help others who might come after me, here are some of them. Most of these lessons I would still agree with although, as we will see later, there are one or two where I decided to take a more nuanced approach when tackling my world record attempt.

1. Fast riders use fast roads

Choosing a route for a race like this is a balancing act, and each rider must consider their own ideal mix of speed, safety and access to facilities. I can't tell you what is the right balance for you. What I can tell you is that the people right up at the sharp end of a race like the Transcontinental are probably taking the bigger, faster roads. They are, to a first approximation, taking the roads you would drive along if you planned the quickest route that avoided motorways.

The benefits of taking main roads are that you are likely to have better surfaces, flatter gradients and regular petrol stations and shops. Major roads are expensive to build and maintain, and so they aren't placed randomly – they pass close to where people live, work and shop; the engineering costs mean these roads do not climb up hills unless it is unavoidable.

Of course, the downside is that the places people live, work and shop are also full of commuters and deliveries, and so traffic is faster, heavier and more voluminous. And a big road that goes a long distance might be a corridor for freight trucks, which are the most intimidating of all.

2. 'Can I do this on the bike?'
This was an approach I brought with me from ultrarunning, where one of the things I was quite good at was not losing too much time in aid stations. There is a lot to do when you reach these checkpoints in a race – filling water bottles, eating food, dressing blisters, putting on or taking off layers of clothing... The temptation is to sit down and hit all these jobs one after the other. However, I quickly learned that I could pull ahead of other competitors by always asking myself 'Could I do this while moving?' Some tasks, like filling water bottles or dressing blisters on my feet, clearly had to be done then and there. But taking off a jacket and stuffing it in my backpack? Eating some of the food I'd just picked up? Tasks like these could be done on the move. It didn't matter if I was only going at walking pace: as long as my speed was greater than zero, it was more efficient to do the task while moving than it was to do it in a chair.

I brought a very similar approach to my Transcontinental ride. Eating? Looking at maps? As long as the road was quiet, these could be done on the bike. Who cares if opening a packet or checking my phone meant I was moving at only 10 kph? I'd still be further down the road than if I had stopped. Pretty much every task was subjected to this question of 'Can I do this on the bike?' Eating, drinking, checking maps, finding hotels... As long as the road was not too steep or busy these were probably fair game.

(2a Something you might start to think you can do on a bike but really cannot: inserting contact lenses.)

(2b Things you can technically do on the bike but probably shouldn't DON'T ASK ME HOW I KNOW: Cleaning your teeth, taking a piss.)

3. Plan each break in advance
As I rode, whenever I thought of a task that needed to be done when next I stopped, I would add it to a running mnemonic so that I would not forget. My internal monologue went something like this:

'When I get to the next shop I need food. And while I'm stopped, I need to oil my chain and check what's making that noise coming from my rear brake. Food, Oil, Brake... FOB. Like a fob-watch. I hope I don't get FOB-bed off in the shop...' And once I had that sort of mental image, I was unlikely to forget my task list.

It was then easy to add extra items into the list by expanding and rearranging the mnemonic. Let's say that my knees started hurting and I decided needed to add painkillers to my shopping list. In this case, I could just add a P into my list of initials and shuffle them around to make, say, PFOB – Planes Fly Over Brussels, or perhaps BPFO – Bored Penguins Fall Over. By creating a mental image of such scenes, I made it easy to remember the list.

(Finally, all those psychology qualifications paid off. Incidentally, if you want to get really good at this sort of memory trick, look up 'method of loci' and 'interactive imagery'. There are ways to make your mnemonics even more memorable than the brief guide I have outlined here.)

4. Hot food is a luxury

When you're tired and hungry it's so nice to sit down and eat a pizza in some unexpected restaurant in the middle of an unfamiliar country. But it takes a long time, and you'll probably ride faster if you can resist the temptation and stick to cold food.

If you absolutely have to stop, can you maximise your use of the time? Can you find a socket in the restaurant where you can charge any electronic appliances? Can you check your route or search for accommodation as you eat?

5. Cities are awful

They are so slow, largely because of all the intersections and traffic lights. I've still not worked out a hard-and-fast rule for this, but if I had to put a figure on it, I reckon the route through a city would have to be something like 50 kilometres shorter before I would go through the urban area rather than go around it.

One nuance here is whether you think you might be able to anticipate what time you will hit the city. If you can be confident you will be there at midnight then it might be a slightly easier crossing than if you hit it during rush hour. Although whatever time you get there, you will likely find you hit the same number of red lights. Indeed, there can be times when crossing a city at night is slower because often traffic lights have sensors that are not triggered by bicycles. This means they will stay red indefinitely if no other traffic comes along.

6. Skipping sleep rapidly becomes a false economy
Daniel Johansson, Michael Wacker, Patrick Miette... These are just some of the Transcontinental riders whom I overtook during my ridiculous Operation Kickass stint – sometimes more than once – but who nevertheless finished the race ahead of me *and* got more sleep along the way. You remember the fable of the tortoise and the hare? This was the real-life version, played out across Serbia and Greece.

I should preface this by saying that cycling or running at night is one of life's great delights – you feel like the most important person in the world as you cruise past sleeping streets and houses, a lone traveller whose secret passage will never be suspected and who has free rein to do whatever they please. And I am the first to admit that pushing right through the night in a multi-day race feels totally badass and hardcore. But you can have too much of a good thing. Eventually, you always slow down during the night. There is a lot of physiology behind this – hormone levels and body temperature change before dawn as part of our circadian rhythms, meaning that, fundamentally, we are built to be asleep during the small hours of the night and your body does not forget this no matter how much you want it to. On long, multi-day rides, there are rare occasions when the all-night push might be the right tactical choice, but more often there comes a time when discretion is the better part of valour.

The simple truth is this: at four in the morning you will be going slower than your usual pace, you will be feeling wretched, and you will be setting yourself up to be slow the following day because you are not rested. It is almost certainly better to grab a bit of sleep and thereby hit your body's reset switch. You will ride a whole lot faster after sunrise and so will make back all the time you spent sleeping, plus a bit extra. Just ask Daniel Johansson, Michael Wacker, Patrick Miette...

The true lessons from the Transcontinental Race

So those were my practical lessons, presented here in the hope you might find them useful if you ever undertake long-distance riding yourself. But what were the real lessons? What did I take away from the experience of such a long, tough race?

Perhaps most importantly, I learned something valuable about how I was able to handle difficulty. Several times during the Transcontinental my plans underwent serious setbacks. All that lost progress in Italy after I took a bad route, the night I had to backtrack in Romania, that period of despair in the Serbian construction site... Looking back as I write this, several years later, I am really pleased with how I coped with these situations. As a way to make up for lost time, Operation Kickass was silly and – I now realise – a counterproductive racing strategy. But more importantly, it was a healthy, humorous reaction to a difficult situation. I had been planning and training for this race for over six months and it had all gone wrong. My strong position in the race had been so unexpected, yet so welcome when it appeared. As I watched it fall away, I might have become angry, or overwhelmed. I might have quit the race and been left forever wondering whether I could have finished. Yet rather than do any of these things, my response when I found myself under pressure was to laugh at the situation and get on with it anyway.

Looking back, I have to tell you that I am very proud of myself for that.

Racing TCR also left me with a deep awe and respect for the human body. Our bodies have been shaped over hundreds of thousands of years so that we are masters of endurance. If all you have done with your body is ask it to engage in a modern Western lifestyle, you have barely begun to explore what it can do. I was regularly stirred into deep emotions at seeing, first hand, what I had been capable of all this time without realising it – how my body could climb mountains, drive itself into deep pits of exhaustion and then, with the briefest of sleeps, begin the whole process again. *I can do anything*, I would think as I rode, magically renewed, into each morning sunrise.

I also gained a new appreciation for the vastness of Europe, and was struck by just how much of the continent is used for growing crops. I had not fully realised how, outside the mountains, most of the countries on this continent are basically a few cities and towns scattered among an otherwise endless patchwork of corn, wheat and sunflowers. I have seen the statistics about how the world continues to become increasingly urban, but it is hard to believe them when you undertake a journey like this. So much of our continent is a vast and largely traditional rural space. It is easy to forget this – both geographically and politically.

There was one other thing that I learned too: something very interesting about the process of dedicating yourself to a difficult task for a long time. It is possible that this was the most profound lesson of all.

'What do you think about when you're riding?'

When you ride big distances, you spend a lot of time with only your own thoughts for company. Yet it is notable how many people talk about these periods of solitude being when their minds most readily find peace. An interesting truth about ultradistance cyclists seems to be that many ride the big miles, in part, because it is the only time they are totally at ease. This is not simply introversion; there is something deeper at play here, linked to the physical act of riding.

The experience is most profound when you race a big distance, as opposed merely to riding it. A race requires you to be fast, and this need for speed is what forces you to ride without reservation or distraction, handing your whole self over to the venture you have chosen. The requirement to be efficient demands that you strip your existence back to its most elemental components: movement, water, food, shelter. This is no hardship: you discover it is a relief to have the complexity of everyday existence lifted from you and replaced by these simple concerns. And are they even truly concerns? There is a sense in which all the important decisions were made in advance when you chose to undertake the journey. Eventually you realise that your deep commitment to the cause of moving quickly offers the chance to pass through into a new state of being in which your waking mind can finally become free from questions. *Where will I go today?* Further along the route, the same as yesterday. *What will I eat?* Whatever I find, just like yesterday. *Where will I sleep?* Let's see where I end up. Hush now. Hush.

All this creates a strange paradoxical state of being. When I ride, my mind is both crowded and empty. The practical part of me churns, thinking all the time about navigation, shops, food, weather and lodging, seeking information about those raw essentials of life and planning dozens of contingencies. But when I look back on any given ride, even one lasting many days, I would struggle to tell you a single thought that passed through my head, because the rest of my mind has been liberated. All of life's needs have been simplified, and then delegated to the fretting part of my mind. This part of me works like the legs on a swan; it has to be there, thrashing unseen beneath the surface, so that the main part of me can glide peaceful and still among its surroundings. And this sense of profound peace would never happen without the need to ride fast. So hush, and enjoy the silence.

Part 3
North Cape 4000

It was late 2017, and Autumn had arrived. As the colder and wetter days swept in, I continued riding as much as I could. While other cyclists hibernated for the year, moving indoors to play video games on turbo trainers in their warm homes, I used my increasingly wintery commutes to toughen me up. They taught me how to put up with discomfort and how to endure grinding into a crippling headwind when all you want is for the journey to be over. I also got valuable practice with problem-solving, such as when my headlamp failed on a dark ride home and I was forced to improvise a replacement. I'm still proud of my solution: I used a bike lock to strap my phone to the handlebars with its camera flash illuminated to make me visible to motorists.

I went into the winter wanting more adventure and wondering how I would build on what I had learned from the TCR. The obvious thing was to enter the race again and try to do better. TCR uses a different set of checkpoints every year, meaning it takes a very different route each time. As such, it would not feel like I was merely doing the same thing all over again. I would also be going into the race with my eyes more open than the previous year and would be able quite directly to compare my new performance with my last, to measure my progress.

But before committing to a second attempt at the TCR, I looked around for other ultradistance races, just to make sure I didn't overlook any opportunities that might appeal even more. I soon came upon the North Cape 4000.

The North Cape 4000 is, very technically, 'not a race', presumably because if it were officially a race there would be issues of liability and insurance. But as I was to discover, for the people who take part it is every bit as much a competition as TCR is. Both events had a core of serious competitors who were fighting one another to finish first, and then a larger pack of people who were not so much racing as undertaking a big personal challenge. The two events were, in all the ways that mattered, the same thing.

The NC4K, as we riders soon started to call it, began in Arco, in the north of Italy, and all the entrants would follow exactly the same predefined 4300-kilometre route up through Europe to the final northernmost tip of the continent at North Cape in Norway. Ah, so *that* is what those bikepackers had been doing with their race numbers in northern Italy the previous year. I found myself fascinated by the logic and simplicity of setting out and then riding continually northward until we literally ran out of continent. I signed up. The fact it was very similar in length to TCR also meant I would be making the most of my experience – I now knew what it felt like to ride that distance and would be better able to prepare myself and manage the whole experience mentally.

The fixed route appealed to me too. One of the highlights of the Transcontinental had been bumping into other riders from time to time. It was a pleasure to roll into a petrol station and spot another rider's bike propped against a wall outside, as though patiently awaiting a companion. These occasional encounters gave a chance to say hello to somebody undergoing the same experiences and to be reminded that my long hours of suffering were part of something bigger. So I was keen on the idea of the fixed route, thinking it would increase the number of times this should happen.

I began the process of getting myself into shape. My training followed a similar form to the previous year: lots of commuting with occasional much longer rides on weekends, particularly on Audax UK events. But feeling instinctively that I needed to stir things up a bit to avoid getting stuck in a rut, I started to do more structured workouts during my commutes. Something I had learned from my running is that, up to a certain point, there are huge gains to be made simply by getting in a large volume of relatively low-intensity exercise. But after a while, you hit a point where this stops helping you improve and more focused efforts are needed.

That January, then, I bit the bullet and bought a power meter for my bike. I am tempted to joke that there is no better device for helping the keen rider to overthink every aspect of their riding, but in fact it was worth every penny. At first, the expense seemed extraordinary, but I soon realised just how valuable this new source of information was – especially as I did plenty of reading to learn how to interpret the meter's output. I was soon able to use it to focus my training and so improve the specific physiological systems I needed. Many of my commutes became interval sessions and often I arrived at work with my face flushed from stinging hard efforts as I worked on pushing up my power threshold or VO2max. Although I never needed to ride that hard in races, these tough efforts would build me up so I could cruise comfortably at faster speeds for longer periods.

I also fell for a startlingly yellow carbon bike made by Whyte after spotting it in a shop in Bath. A test ride revealed a frame that felt gloriously stiff and responsive compared to my existing bike and I committed to buying one the next day. A few months later I delved into the dregs of my bank account and bought some hand-made deep-section carbon aero wheels for it. I took a chance by buying these from London wheelbuilder Judith Stayer after speaking to her on the phone and finding her knowledge and enthusiasm immediately convincing. ('As long as they're race-winning wheels,' said Louise when I told her. I nodded nervously.)

My confidence in the build-up to the event was boosted by performing well in two challenging rides. At the start of

May I entered a low-key bikepacking competition called the TransWales race. This was organised by Mostyn Brown who, by coincidence, had ridden right next to me on the climb up the Kapelmuur at the start of the TCR the previous summer. TransWales saw a bunch of riders gather at midnight in Anglesey in the north of Wales and then ride as fast as possible to Cardiff in the south of the country, each taking whatever route we liked with the proviso that we shared time-stamped photographs of ourselves at a series of dams along the way. I comfortably finished first, which pleased me greatly.

My final shakedown was the Three Coasts 600 Audax in June. Here I cracked off 617 hilly kilometres in less than 23 hours of riding (and under 27.5 hours in total, including eating, repairs and so on). It was another big shot of self-belief, reassuring me that my training had worked. I rounded everything off with a great little 200-km ride with a friend called Mark Townsend a fortnight before the race. Mark lives close to me in Bristol but, curiously, we first met in Greece, when he was helping run things at the end of the Transcontinental. Our ride out across the Somerset Levels and back up Cheddar Gorge felt easy and fun after all the training. I perhaps didn't appreciate at the time how this was to be my last ride without any time pressure.

All this saw me travel to the start line at Arco feeling there was not a whole lot more I could have done to prepare, which was a good feeling. But as soon as I got there, I found this did little to help with my imposter syndrome. It was impossible to look around the other competitors and their shiny bikes and not feel intimidated. There were even sponsored, semi-professional riders there. Their gleaming new machines with wheels custom-made for the event worried me greatly. But, the nagging self-doubt aside, I enjoyed the experience of waiting around at the start with the other riders. Ever since I was running, I've always enjoyed the hanging-around-and-shooting-the-breeze part of races. It's rare to spend time with other people who truly understand

what I do. More concretely, there are very few opportunities in life to learn ingenious new ways of carrying spare
spokes, and so I took full advantage of these chats in Arco.

Then the ride began – a new battle of 4300 kilometres.
For a few kilometres we riders were led out of Arco at a sedate pace behind a local cyclist until, on the outskirts of town,
he pulled aside and we were unleashed to begin the ride
proper. A group of about twenty of us immediately got very
competitive, pushing hard, gauging one another, flexing our
muscles and hammering the climbs – including one notably
challenging slope that ascended brutally from the shore of
Lake Garda up into the hills. The pace was punishing. After
a couple of hours we were riding along a long false flat on a
wide track and I found myself with a difficult choice: continue to push harder than I felt I could sustain so that I
could continue to enjoy the aerodynamic advantage of being in this peloton, or ride more easily but lose this advantage. I went for the second option: I dropped my effort by
about 30 Watts and very slowly watched the pack pull away
from me. It was hard to do. Watching the other riders' re-
ceding backs immediately made me ask if I was fooling myself to think I could ever have been competitive here.

But, difficult as it was to watch such a large group leave
me behind, it proved to be the right decision. As the day
unfolded beneath a sweltering sun, I started to reel in
people as they cracked from the effort of trying to keep up
and fell off the back of this pack one by one. It was reassuring, and a good lesson in sticking to the plan and not worrying about the other competitors too much. Four thousand
kilometres is a long way to ride at somebody else's pace.

Even after I dropped my power, the early effort still carried a price – especially with the heat we were riding in. We
had one big climb that day, taking us over the Reschenpass
to get to the northern side of the Alps. The final part of this
ascent was exactly the sort of switchback road you probably
associate with the high mountains, but the bulk of the climb
was far less exciting and we spent hours on a long gradual

ascent. I'd always prefer an honest slope of around 7% or 8% that gets the climbing over with, rather than some gradual slope that spins it out for ages. This climb went on for over 80 kilometres, ascending on exactly the kind of 1-2% gradients that I find so tedious. When I eventually hit a proper slope, up the last 10 kilometres of the climb to the Reschenpass, I couldn't really enjoy it because I started to pay for the early hard effort of the day. My legs lacked power. Rider after rider passed me as if I were barely moving, which was a serious blow to morale. I didn't realise it at the time, but these people sailing past me would be a big feature of my life over the coming days as we fell into a cluster of competitors all moving at roughly the same pace, leapfrogging one another over and over. But on that climb, I did not know that: I just knew I was being passed by a lot of people and I didn't like it one bit.

It didn't help that the people overtaking me on that first major climb all looked like such heroic riders: rangy Austrian Markus Zimmerman glided by first, looking entirely at home on the ascent; Italian Paolo Botti then passed me, looking every inch the hardman that he later proved to be. Perhaps the most striking of all was a big bearded blond Czech rider called Aleš Zavoral. To get a picture of what it feels like to be passed by Aleš, just imagine seeing Thor out on a day ride from Valhalla. These three and more left me gasping on that first big climb. It felt an ominous start to such a huge undertaking.

The comeback kid

So here's the short version of the entire North Cape 4000: I went out too hard at the start, spent all of the second day feeling a total mess and being passed by other riders, but I still went on to finish in first place. I don't know if you will ever see a stronger example of the most basic principle of endurance sport: if you just keep moving, everything can come good eventually.

I woke at the start of the second day feeling dreadful. I had snatched a few hours of shitty sleep in a shop doorway in a small Austrian town called Wiesing. It was a bad place to sleep but I had been forced to make a quick decision when it started raining around midnight and I had been unable to find anywhere better. I was particularly disappointed by the church that stood prominently in the centre of the town. Weren't churches all meant to have porches that can shelter weary travellers? But I circled right around this one and there was zero shelter of any sort. And so I ended up in this doorway, tossing and turning under a bright security light, woken every few minutes by the surprisingly high volume of motor traffic passing through this nowhere town in the small hours of the night, the vehicles' tyres crashing loud on the wet road.

It was no surprise, then, that the second day found me weak and ineffectual. The early hard efforts on Day One had drained my legs and my disturbed sleep had done little to refresh me. The numbers staring up from my computer confirmed with brutal objectivity that I was producing less power than I would have expected, and at a higher heart rate than I would like. I abandoned any hopes of being near the front of the pack and resigned myself to the new ambition of merely finishing the ride. 'Just keep turning the pedals,' I told myself over and over. 'You're not going to do well, but you still need to do your best.' There were low points that day where I asked myself why I was bothering with this at all. Why not just catch a train? I could be home tomorrow. What helped me push these negative thoughts aside was the knowledge I had gained from my previous races. I knew such moments were always going to come along. I had felt bad on many occasions before, and it had always passed eventually. I just had to keep moving.

I pushed through the sleepy food desert that is Bavaria on a Sunday, had a close encounter with a massive wasp nest, and then climbed two big hills to drop into Czechia. Under the soft warm blanket of the summer night I had a great sleep on the roadside, lulled unconscious by the gentle sounds of water birds on a nearby lake. The next morning my alarm woke me before dawn. I immediately felt dramatically better than I had the day before. As the orange sun climbed over the horizon and began to warm the tarmac, I reflected on how right I had been to keep on moving and to resist the nagging voices of self-doubt. It never always gets worse.

I blasted right across Czechia that day, for a total of 297 kilometres. Like all big cities, Prague slowed me down a lot, but I was able to take comfort from the knowledge that all the other riders had to follow exactly the same route and so would experience similar delays. The centre of Prague was the first checkpoint of the ride, and I was pleased to find I arrived there in fifth place, only shortly behind the number four rider. I wasted no time, and got back on the road immediately. This was partly to try to chase down the rider ahead of me, and partly a ploy: I wanted the checkpoint volunteers to tell the riders behind me how strong I had looked, and how easily I rode straight off again after getting my brevet card stamped. I thought it might help demoralise and deter anybody who felt like trying to take me on.

The third day ended at an altitude of over 1000 metres, in a touristy village called Horní Malá Úpa right on the Czech-Polish border. I wanted to press on further but my phone, lights and battery pack were all low on power and so I czeched (sorry) into a hostel to recharge. For some reason, the hostel staff were only able to provide me with a small mattress on the floor of a huge empty room in the attic, but I didn't care. I plugged in my chargers, set an alarm and fell into a sweaty and not entirely restful sleep.

Sleeping at altitude is a mistake on races like this, because it means you have to start the next day descending before you have a chance to warm up. I knew this, but had no real choice thanks to my flat batteries. Sure enough, my pre-dawn start the next day saw me shivering and miserable as I dropped hundreds of metres through frigid air without turning the pedals at all. Once down, though, Poland started to wake up and, finally, so did I. With a thousand kilometres under my belt, my body caught up with the idea of what it had agreed to and started really to race. My blood coursing with new-found energy, I cracked off 427 kilometres across Poland despite some shocking road surfaces. I continued strong until a little after midnight, when I started to feel weary and heavy. Despite the urgency of my fatigue, I could find nowhere to bivvy. The woodlands thrummed with mosquitoes and the roadside bus shelters were full of dirt and had no benches. I looked hard, but could find nowhere I was prepared to sleep – and my standards were far from high by that point. Eventually, at 2 in the morning, I rolled towards a small town called Łowicz. *I'll get to the other side of this town and then I'll just have to bivvy in the first flat place I can find*, I thought. *If the mosquitoes eat me then so be it – there's no way I can go any further.*

The Audax Gods had different ideas, however. As I rolled into the sleeping town I spotted a neon 'Hotel' sign glowing in the street. *There's no way this is going to be open at this time of night*, I thought. But the door swung inwards at my touch, and the kindly night manager gave me a room at a good price. I showered days of road dirt from my body and then sprawled across the bed with a huge grin on my face.

IW and AZ

Checkpoint 2 was in the heart of Warsaw, so it was another slow ride through honking traffic chaos before I could get back into the countryside and make some real progress. Happily, the ride into the city provided one of those rare and glorious periods of ecstatic flow that are the athlete's reward for their dedication. As I rode through the suburbs, I felt myself sink into the bicycle and become entirely connected with the act of pedalling. Each stroke of my legs was perfect. I handled the bike through corners with unimprovable precision, as though I were running on rails constructed by the finest Swiss engineer. My heart sang, and then so did I. I felt the usual low-grade grief when the moment finally passed.

I believed I was still in fifth place, but it was hard to be certain. The Warsaw checkpoint was in the tourist information centre and while the staff there were happy to stamp our cards, they were not specifically attached to the race. The young man who dealt with me said he thought I might be fifth, but had only started his shift a short time earlier so could not be sure.

The race tracking system was also unhelpful. Ultracycling races usually use tracking devices made by a company called Spot, which read your position and speed from GPS signals every few minutes, then upload this information through telecommunications satellites. They are great devices, and work almost anywhere on Earth without having to rely on patchy mobile phone networks, but they are fairly expensive to own. Motivated by good intentions, the organisers of the North Cape 4000 used a race tracking system that allowed riders who did not possess a Spot tracker to upload their position every few minutes using an app on their phones. Whether the data came from a tracker or a phone, each of us was marked on the map by a big dot that contained our initials. These crawled slowly across the map, showing the world where we each were almost in real time. My 'IW' marker sat amongst the cluster of riders up near the front. A long tail of dots already stretched hundreds of kilometres behind us.

Unfortunately, the way the organisers had allowed riders to use a phone app to update their position meant that riders' dots could stop updating on the tracker if they were in an area where phone coverage was poor. More prosaically, it also meant people could prevent the race tracker from showing their positions simply by turning their phones off. At least two of the people near the front of the race were taking advantage of this. Whereas my map marker, and the markers of most other riders, updated its position on the map of Europe every five or ten minutes, these two riders would apparently stay immobile for hours and then, suddenly, their markers would jump 100 kilometres or more. It meant knowing where they were was impossible. This behaviour was deeply unsporting. It is in the spirit of these races that everybody shares their location with their competitors so that each rider can make informed tactical decisions. To opt out of this while still having access to other riders' positions is to have a substantial and unfair advantage. I began to harbour a simmering resentment of the dots labelled MW and DR. I passed the hours thinking of various rude terms that these initials might represent.

The weather had turned hot again, so sweat was clamping my jersey to my skin as I rolled into a petrol station and found another competitor's bike leaning against the wall outside. I knew from the race tracker that this was Thor from the first day: AZ – Aleš Zavoral. The big Czech greeted me warmly as I arrived and the two of us chatted easily as we ate and drank on the forecourt – we lamented the heat, the mosquitoes, and the rough Polish roads that looked as though they had been resurfaced from orbit. When we had finished our drinks and ice creams it seemed natural to ride on together. Without our having to discuss it, we started to roll along side-by-side, continuing our discussion. Later, as the heat of the day reached a crescendo, Aleš and I sat on the kerb outside a village shop, eating ice creams and toasting each other with cold bottles of beer that felt practically illicit in the setting of a race.

Night fell, close and humid. A vast cloud of mosquitoes appeared and followed us everywhere. Neither Aleš nor I found we had any appetite to bivvy if it meant getting eaten by these pests. We stopped in a small town north of Białystok to ask if there was a hotel anywhere, but had no joy. At the next town we found four young men drinking beer in the town square after midnight and asked again if there was anywhere we could stay. One of the young men picked up his phone, pressed a single button and then spoke for perhaps fifteen seconds. 'There is motel on main road,' he said, lowering the phone. 'They have room. They keep room for you, but you must be quick. Is five kilometres. Motel is big. Many lights. Easy to see.'

There was no way he had arranged all that in such a quick phone call. I wasn't even sure he had really dialled a number. He and his boozy mates were no doubt sniggering about their prank the moment we rode away. But, lacking any better ideas, Aleš and I started along the main road in the direction indicated. We rode five kilometres in total darkness, Aleš in front and me behind, trucks flashing past our shoulders. It was the biggest and busiest road I had been on so far in this race.

There was no motel. Of course there wasn't.

We rode another kilometre, then another, and another. Eventually I shouted ahead for Aleš to stop. Over the noise of the traffic I bellowed 'How far are we going to ride before we admit there's no motel?'.

'Let's look at the map,' Aleš said.

I pulled out my phone and at once saw that we were heading in completely the wrong direction. Bollocks. We turned around and rode the eight kilometres back to the town where the man had given us directions, and then carried on past it. Five kilometres later, exactly as promised, we found a big, brightly lit truckers' motel by the side of the road. We went inside and found that, sure enough, they had a room that they were saving for us. I'm sorry for ever doubting you, Man in the Street.

Lycra and Lamé

Here is the tweet I sent from Poland:

So I've ended up sharing a trucker motel room with a guy I basically met this morning. A motel room with gold lamé bedspreads. You can't say that life is boring when you do competitive ultracycling... #NC4K #NorthCape4000

Aleš jumped in the shower while I grabbed two big bottles of beer from reception, and then we toasted each other again before I had a shower and climbed into one of the two gilded beds, each with its own dusty bike leaning against the adjacent wall. As I tweeted at the time, this kind of racing certainly opens you up to new experiences.

But, for all the fun and camaraderie of my time with Aleš, I awoke the next morning feeling apprehensive about how best to continue. The two of us had fallen into riding together quite naturally. We hadn't even discussed keeping each other company; it had just happened. Having a companion for a while had been unexpectedly enjoyable, but it was easy to see we were slowing each other down. This is inevitable when people ride together, and explains why the teams of two that are allowed in the Transcontinental Race are always beaten by solo riders, even with all the aerodynamic drafting advantages the pairs should have.[4] With two people, the little jobs that demand a roadside halt, such as tightening a loose piece of luggage or removing a jacket, double in number, eating into precious riding time. The

4 For the record, Aleš and I scrupulously avoided drafting one another! We rode side-by-side, or with clear distance between us.

time spent at food stops goes up too: having company in-
troduces a new dynamic of 'Does he look ready to leave?
No, he looks like he wants to stay here a bit longer; I'd better wait a while' that is absent when you are on your own.
Much as I was enjoying Aleš's company, it was clear we
were not helping each other ride fast. And this was, after all,
a race – one that we were somewhere near the front of.

I was dressed and ready first, and sat back on my bed to
wait for Aleš to finish his tasks. I wanted to leave but – being
British – was so worried that I might cause offence with this
suggestion that I was resigning myself to sticking with him
despite my better judgement. Aleš seemed to read my
thoughts.

'You should go,' he said, looking up from the bag he was
sorting through.

'Are you sure?' I replied, perhaps a little too quickly.

'Yes, it will be better for the race if we go separately.'

We hugged, and I turned to the door. 'I suspect you'll
catch me up before long,' I said as I pushed my bike out of
the room. But I wasn't to see my bedroom companion
again.

Out on the road, pedalling reasonably hard so as not to
make things too easy for Aleš, it wasn't long before I began
climbing into some gently rolling green hills that took me
over the border into Lithuania. It was the first time I had
been in the Baltic States. At once, Lithuania seemed to have
more everyday niceties than Poland. The public spaces in
Poland felt sparse and functional. A Polish bus shelter was
literally a shelter. There would be no seats, no litter bin, no
timetable. In comparison, it felt as though there was a
greater generosity in Lithuania: suddenly there were picnic
tables by the roadside, benches, playgrounds for children,
public toilets. The warm, still air became filled with butter-
flies. And then...

'That's Russia!' I said out loud.

Just after Vištytis the road crooked westward and began to
run right up alongside the high-security fence that separ-

ated me from the Russian exclave of Kaliningrad. Having grown up through the final part of the Cold War, it was striking to turn a corner and see our old enemy literally within a stone's throw of the road. Dozens of security cameras followed my passing as I snapped surreptitious photographs of Russian trees from the bike. Across the road, on the Lithuanian side, I was watched by eerie abandoned windmills in the fields. These seemed to follow my passage along the quiet road like reproachful sentinels.

Dirt and pain

The race turned around for me the following day. What am I saying? *Life* turned around for me that day. I started out as somebody who just did long rides for fun; I ended the day as somebody with the drive to win. I made a choice that day and it changed everything.

I was back on the road in Lithuania before dawn, after a short sleep in a hotel attached to a windmill in Šeduva. I left the hotel before breakfast was served, but quickly found an unexpected coffee vending machine thrumming to itself in a sleeping street in the middle of the town. The hot drink at least gave me the illusion of being fuelled as I headed out into the darkness.

It was not long before the slow sun appeared and another hot day settled on the land. As I rode, storks studiously ignored me from their giant nests on top of the power-cable poles that sat along the dusty roads. I clucked and called, but held no interest for these fey creatures. Storks always make me wonder if aliens are already amongst us and we have been overlooking them all along.

Three hours later I was over another border into Latvia, where I faced one of the biggest challenges of this event. For a substantial stretch through this country, the route chosen by the race organisers followed a shockingly poor dirt road. Late in the run-up to the event, they had conceded that we riders could avoid this section if we liked, as long as we didn't use dangerous major roads. Taking this option to avoid the dirt roads would add quite a few kilometres to the ride, however, so the choice was between comfort or speed.

At any point in the past, I would probably have chosen comfort. But something changed that day. I decided to take advantage of my strong placing in the race by trying to get into the lead. Why not? I thought. Why not take that new, extra step? So far I had been cruising comfortably, and that had put me somewhere near the front of the race. But I was in such a good position more because I was well trained than because I was making any special effort. But now, I thought, how about I take that jump into the unknown, and go from merely riding to truly *racing*?

Right there in Latvia, I literally and metaphorically stood at a crossroads. To my left was comfort and familiarity, and ahead was risk and reward. Faced with this choice between ease and speed, fired up by a new-found killer instinct, I faced forward and I chose speed.

The road was brutal – far worse than any other dirt or gravel that I have ridden before or since. The surface had formed into an endless procession of washboard ridges that hammered me through the handlebars. My vision blurred and my wrists screamed as I fought to keep the bike under control while my front wheel bucked and bounced. Riding slow enough that there was no pain meant riding at walking pace. Pain was the only option.

Half-way through the gravel section the route dropped into a small dusty village that sat at a crossroads. I had no phone service in Latvia: my phone company had no arrangement with any of the Latvian networks and so even though my own satellite tracker had continued to tell everybody else where I was, I had been unable to check on the other riders since crossing the border. I bought a cold drink from a shop to wash the dust from my mouth and used the shop's WiFi to check the race tracker as I drank. There was still some uncertainty about where everybody was, thanks to the riders who were not updating their positions regularly, but I was nevertheless able to see something useful: of the four riders who were definitely ahead of me, three had detoured around the entire gravel section. The one remaining rider ahead of me had, shortly before my arrival, reached the village in which I now stood and then detoured westwards to take sealed roads rather than endure the second half of the planned gravel section. Clearly he had found the surface so tough that he had decided to take the hit of riding extra kilometres to avoid further dirt-road suffering.

If I could out-tough my opponent, I had a chance to get ahead.

I hit the second part of the road, coughing on dust trails kicked up by the drivers who roared past in their cars. After leaving the small village I was again unable to check the race tracker, but scenting the chance to get ahead in the race, I blindly threw everything I had at the effort and rode at a frankly ridiculous pace for the conditions. My body was pummelled and thrashed. Between coughing fits, I screamed curses at the uncaring road. *Fuck you, road! Fuck you fuck you FUCK YOU!* Every time I felt I must finally be at the end of this section, I turned a corner and found a new stretch of shattered rock surface disappearing into the distance through the trees. I began to resign myself to never feeling stillness again.

And then, gloriously, I emerged from a patch of woodland to find my dirt track joined a smooth tarmacadamed road. I dismounted so I could run my fingertips over its surface, so overjoyed was I finally to be through the dirt section.

And, perhaps best of all, I thought I might now be in the lead.

Dotwatchers

An ultradistance cycle race is an exercise in solipsistic aloneness. A rider spends all day inside their own head, entirely focused on the challenge of moving as fast and as far as possible. The race becomes so absorbing that it is easy to forget the rest of the world exists.

It is also easy to forget that the markers crawling across the map on the race tracking website are not only there so the competitors can keep tabs on their rivals: those markers are also closely followed by the dotwatchers – the spectators who follow events the only way they can when their chosen sport unfolds over thousands of kilometres. It is a strange, dislocating feeling to be riding along in the middle of the night and suddenly to remember that people on the other side of the world might be sitting at home watching you move. The knowledge of the dotwatchers' presence can be a reassuring comfort to the lost or lonely rider in an ultradistance race. They also act as a check on the would-be cheat who might be tempted to take a short-cut or obtain forbidden help. The dotwatchers are able to zoom in on a rider's marker until the specific hotel or shop they have visited can be determined. They can see exactly how fast each rider travels. There is nowhere to hide from their gaze and it is impossible to know when they might be looking. Honesty is the only option.

The unexpected appearance of a dotwatcher in real life is one of the great delights to be found during an ultracycling race.

I first experienced this on the Transcontinental Race. Riding down a mountain in Italy I heard the thrumming burr of another bicycle's freewheel and glanced up as a man pulled alongside me on a shiny black bicycle. 'You must be Ian,' he said. 'I've been watching you.' A day or two later I crossed a narrow bridge into the Slovenian city of Ptuj to find a young woman waving me down and wanting to say hello. I came to love these encounters for how they pulled me out of the immediacy of the race, reminding me that I wasn't just out on yet another long ride: I was part of a much bigger event that had captivated an unknown crowd of strangers.

I had another such encounter on the NC4K in Latvia. Late in the afternoon I emerged from a supermarket in Sigulda with my arms full of bottles and packets to find a man photographing me with a large camera from across the car park. He turned out to be a friendly local journalist who had been following the race and was hoping to photograph all the riders as they came through his town. He explained that I was the second rider to come through (dammit!) but that I was only a short distance behind the leader (yay!). He followed me to the railway station where he took photographs of me balanced on my bike near a sculpture, then reappeared to take more pictures as I climbed a hill out of the town.

And then, late that afternoon, somewhere in the north of Latvia, around 2500 kilometres into the race, I overtook the leader.

The thousand-mile breakaway

I hadn't expected to lead the race.

Yes, of course I had *wanted* to lead the race, and yes, I had *tried* to lead – especially since being struck by the opportunity that the dirt-road section provided earlier that day – but I had never truly expected I would. Why would I? This was only my second race and I had finished quite some way down the pack in the last one. Finding myself now in first position, I had a moment of indecision. The day was drawing to a close and I was apparently just a short distance ahead of the next rider, but I was unable to track his position until I got some phone signal. I had to do something decisive.

And that's how I began a thrilling, nerve-wracking chase through the night across two countries.

The roads improved considerably as I crossed the border into Estonia just after sunset, and a couple of kilometres later I finally had a signal on my phone for the first time since Lithuania. Once the pent-up deluge of texts, emails and other messages calmed down, I called Louise as I turned north and barrelled down the edge of Highway 6, chasing the shaky pool of light cast by my headlamp. I explained to her that I had a big problem. We riders were expected to take a ferry from Tallinn to Helsinki to get across the Gulf of Finland for the final stretch of the ride up through Finland and Norway to North Cape, but this process was far from simple. The ferries had to be booked in advance, which meant you had to know what time you wanted to sail. This, in turn, meant you had to know what time you would be at the docks in Tallinn: not an easy thing to know with any accuracy when you are on a bicycle two hundred kilometres away. To make things even more complicated, there were three separate companies that ran ferries across the Gulf, each with its own sailing schedule. So misjudging my arrival would mean potentially waiting many hours for the next crossing while other riders caught up with me – perhaps even overtaking me, if they made a better choice of ferry operator. It was an agonising series of uncertainties.

Thankfully – by luck as much as anything – I judged it right. Despite two very anxious hours of waiting at the ferry terminal in Tallinn, I managed to get on my boat ahead of the next riders and maintained most of my hard-won advantage into the final stretch of the race. As soon as I boarded the ferry I paid extra for a cabin to try and snatch an hour's sleep, but despite feeling shattered after 565 continuous kilometres of riding I lay there restless in the darkness. Still, it was good to be still.

All too soon our arrival in Helsinki was announced and I pulled myself vertical and continued riding. Once out of the capital, I headed up through the country for another 187 kilometres before hitting a heavy rain storm. Since Latvia, where a rough road had torn my rear tyre, I had been riding a seven-Euro tyre bought from a backstreet bike shop. At first I had struggled to feel any difference between this cheap tyre and the expensive handmade tyre it had replaced. But the rain in Finland revealed the difference all too starkly when a couple of frightening skids showed me that the Latvian tyre had all the wet-weather grip of a buttered oyster. Thankfully, just as the storm really began to come down, I spotted a small basic hotel in Sysmä, and they had a room free. I had ridden a total of 752 kilometres between sleep stops.

It was that day, when I aggressively pushed myself to ride 752 kilometres in a single burst of riding to snatch and hold the lead of a race, that I first began to realise what sort of rider I might be. Finally, perhaps, I could remove the large invisible '*Bad at sport*' sign I had worn around my neck for the past 30 years.

It was also then when I first started to appreciate the gulf that exists between riding and racing. It is one thing to ride hard, but to go from riding hard to riding right at my limits meant crossing a line that I had previously not even glimpsed. That extra few per cent change in speed means a doubling or tripling of the physical and mental demands. To reach deep within yourself and throw everything you have at a monumental physical task is to move to a different plane of existence. It was a new discovery to me at the time, and as that day ended in Sysmä I was still only seeing the first inklings of what it meant to go all-out in sport. I pushed harder than I ever had before, and new depths of my own passion and ability were revealed to me as a reward.

Why does it have to be a race?

Why not just ride?

This is a good question. Why not just load some luggage onto a bike and go for a nice leisurely journey? Cycle touring is a great way to see the world, experiencing a country's landscape and people with an intimacy unknown to most travellers. Cycle touring shows you both the breadth and the depth of a place, exposing you to new locales every day in a way that lets you understand the scale and arrangement of the land. Those in planes, trains and automobiles miss everything; those on foot travel too slowly to see any real change from one day to the next; it is only the cyclist who travels at exactly the right pace, right at the sweet-spot where there is both variety and connectedness. Why ruin this by blasting across a continent with your head down, seeing nothing?

There are as many answers to this as there are competitive long-distance riders.

For me, racing provides a way to test myself and see what I am capable of. I am not an unusually fast cyclist, and if I were, I would find satisfaction in criteriums or other short, sharp races where I can enjoy the immediate thrill of jostling wheel-to-wheel and making split-second tactical decisions. But my endurance physiology – more the result of genetics than training – means I could never be among the best in that sort of racing. More importantly, I could never perform to the best of my potential in that sort of racing. This is a far better ambition: few people can aspire to be among the best in the world at something, but we can all aspire to maximise our potential. And so, if I want to learn what I am truly capable of and see how I behave when pushed, my circumstances mean that I have to do this in long, time-consuming races lasting days or weeks. In many ways, I wish this were not so. Being an ultradistance racer means I can enter very few races each year – or even over my career – as each is such a large commitment. These races swallow time, as each lasts a matter of weeks and there are huge recovery periods afterwards. They also swallow money: the costs of travel, accommodation and equipment soon mount up.

The other reason I race across continents, rather than tour them, is that I think racing provides a legitimacy for the adventure and excess. If I were just some lone person on a bike pushing himself too hard, eating crap from roadside shops and sleeping in bus shelters, that would all be a bit weird and hard to justify. But if I am a *racer*... well, that's a very different matter. As long as we accept that sport matters – and our society clearly does – then the monomania and bizarre behaviour needed to move as fast as possible are not just excused or explained, they are now *necessary*.

I know that many people do not understand this. And perhaps there will come a time when I too wish to slow down and better enjoy the places through which I travel rather than have the landscape pass by in a blur, placing quality over quantity at last. But for now, to ride slowly feels like the bigger missed opportunity.

Freezing in the midnight sun

Racing northwards up Finland over the next three days was like climbing a mountain from its base to beyond its treeline. At first, in the south of the country, I cruised amongst towering firs and pines and then, as my legs spun the pedals for one hour after another, I saw the forests thin and shrink until, by the time I reached the top of Norway, the once-mighty woodlands were reduced to a scattering of stumpy brown *krumholz*. Eventually, as I neared North Cape, the trees would disappear altogether to reveal a barren and magnificent polar landscape grazed by silent herds of white reindeer.

But that was still to come. That first full day of Finland saw me trying to cement my new-found status as race leader with another big day of riding: 465 kilometres from Sysmä up to the substantial northern city of Oulu. Riding such a long day at this stage in the race was made easier by the pressure of being chased. I was constantly aware of the other riders nipping at my heels and this motivated me to keep on moving. I was pretty ruthless with myself, not permitting myself anything more than minimal rest.

My focus on the other front-runners also meant I continued to be driven to distraction by those riders whose dots were updating only every few hours because they were turning their phones off. I kept running through mental calculations, and plotting routes on Google Maps to try to guess these riders' average speeds from the occasional locations that were visible to me. 'Okay so he was *here* at 0920 and now he's *here* at 1445. Google makes that 132 kilometres, which means he's averaging about 24.5 kph including rest stops, which means...' This was not a relaxing process, and after a while I had to stop myself from doing it. It was making me stressed, and all the fiddling with my phone to monitor my opponents, and to do the mapping and calculations, was slowing me down. *All I can do is ride as fast as possible*, I told myself, setting to it with renewed effort. *Knowing where they are won't actually change that.* But stopping myself from worrying about my competitors was easier said than done.

By this stage, my body was in a state of managed collapse. All the exertion of the race had produced overtraining effects, which meant I had no top-end energy system left at all. Usually, when I am rested, my easy cruising efforts see my heart rate somewhere between 115 and 125, climbing much higher to provide more blood when I push hard. When I got onto the bike each morning through Finland, my heart rate rose to 110 and stayed at exactly that level all day, regardless of how hard I tried to ride. Sprinting, or riding hard up a hill, were no longer options – my heart had nothing extra to give. Any attempts to raise my exertion just led to laboured breathing and no real change in the power I could put into the pedals. If I really pushed myself, my heart might just manage to squeeze out 112 beats per minute, all the while letting me know how much it resented those additional two beats with a hollow feeling of strengthlessness. I had just one effort level and I had to learn to use it for everything: climbs, descents, hundreds of kilometres of pan-flat taiga.

After Oulu I set my sights on the race's final checkpoint in Rovaniemi. This small city sits directly on the Arctic Circle, which excited me greatly. The place has made itself a tourist niche by presenting itself as the 'official' home of Father Christmas, and the checkpoint was amongst the cluster of red buildings designed to funnel visitors' money into local pockets through this wheeze. I got there towards the end of the afternoon, just after the centre had closed, so I had to make do with taking a photograph of my bike leaning against the Arctic Circle sign before pressing on. No meeting with St Nick for me, alas. But I was feeling good. I had a big stash of food from a supermarket in Rovaniemi and was prepared to ride well into the sunlit Arctic night to make this yet another long day.

Unfortunately, my plans were thrown off by weird climatic conditions. At about 0200 the temperature had dropped to -1 Celsius. This was a temperature I would not even think about on my commutes through the previous winter, but for some reason I could not explain, -1 Celsius felt way colder up here beyond Rovaniemi than it had back home. It felt more like -10 or -15.

I had already covered myself with items from my saddlebag: arm warmers and leg warmers; a thermal undershirt; a thermal gilet; my rain jacket. Gloves, obviously. By this point I was wearing the same clothes that had happily handled -1 Celsius in the past, but here I was shivering as though naked. The conditions were hard to explain: when I stood still, I felt okay, but as soon as I started to ride and the air moved over my body, it felt unimaginably cold. I continued to stop at regular intervals to delve into my saddle-bag for further protection. A windproof jacket went on over the waterproof; a neckwarmer was wrapped around my face like a bandanna. Eventually I ended up with my sleeping bag swaddled around my body beneath both jackets, but still I was freezing as I rode. With no more shots left in the locker, I found some old magazines in a bus shelter and stuffed my leg warmers and sleeves with pages torn from these. They helped slightly, but still I was shivering.

Eventually, just north of a town called Torvinen, beneath an unfamiliar sun in the small hours of the night, I was forced to climb into my bivvy bag and take shelter underneath a low bush. My last action upon lying down, and my first action upon waking a few hours later, was to check the race tracker. I slumped with relief when I saw the cold had forced my opponents to stop too.

North Cape

At the front of the race, still fighting to retain my position ahead of the other riders, I was starting to feel hunted. There could be no rest or peace for the fugitive. Every moment was spent worrying about my progress and how I might be losing ground to my competitors. After all this time spent in the lead, and all the effort it had required to stay there, I couldn't help but think about how dispiriting it would be to be overtaken in these final stretches of the race. At times I even found myself rehearsing possible excuses for if this should happen. 'It was all going well but then...' I was disappointed to find myself doing this, and tried to distract myself from such thoughts.

Aleš was behind me, nipping at my heels, as were a few other strong riders who had passed me during my slow Alpine climb on day one, including Markus Zimmerman and Paulo Botti. Miguel Vilacha was also there, whom I had first met on the train to Athens at the end of TCR. But my regular checks of the race tracker were most troubled by the marker labelled 'DR'. It was one of the dots that was updating irregularly and infrequently, making the rider's progress maddeningly difficult to chart. But despite all the uncertainty, one thing slowly and troublingly became clear: unlike all the other riders, who either remained a fixed distance behind me or who were slowly dropping back, DR was ever so gradually catching me up.

This was the penultimate day of my race, and I was feeling the effects of pushing so hard – not least because of the mental and physical pressure that DR was placing on me. Towards the end of the day, Andrea, one of the the race organisers from Arco, caught up with me in his distinctive white car. He pulled alongside and, as I continued to ride, he leaned out of the passenger window so we could exchange greetings and thoughts about the race. I was feeling light-headed from the rush of food after a big blow-out in one of Finland's very last supermarkets a short time earlier. After chatting to Andrea for a few moments, I decided to mention the thing that was bothering me.

'A couple of these other riders keep turning their trackers off. It's not really fair, is it?' I said.

'You mean D–––?' laughed the Italian. 'Ha ha, don't you worry about him! He took a shortcut back in Latvia. We're going to give him a big time penalty. You're fine.'

You might have told me sooner, I thought, contemplating how much more relaxing the past couple of days would have been. But despite coming late, this was welcome news. Discounting DR, I reckoned I was about 6 or 8 hours ahead of Aleš, who was still the next rider behind me. That might sound like a good margin, but at the time it seemed worryingly narrow after so many days of riding. All I could think about was how easily this lead could get eaten up by a mechanical problem, or some other unforeseen calamity. I couldn't let up my effort for a moment, no matter how great the toll on my mind and body.

Along a slow, rolling and entirely deserted road, I crossed the border into Norway where I grabbed a short and blisteringly expensive sleep in a hotel in Karasjok. I almost burst into tears after clopping my bike to the outbuilding where I had been directed, only to discover that I could not find my room and had to walk all the way back to reception to clarify the directions. *I really really need to be unconscious right now*, was all I could think. But, feeling chased, I could not allow myself to take more than three hours' sleep. Or so I thought. When my alarm went off after those three hours, I felt so bleakly broken that I checked the tracker and then permitted myself another hour in bed – something I had never done up to that point. Even after that decadent lie-in, I had such huge bags under my eyes that I could barely push them out of the way to get my contact lenses in.

The morning – my last! – was bright and cold when I left the hotel. I took a photograph of my shadow climbing the hill out of Karasjok and tweeted it with the caption 'Let's do this'. The knowledge that the suffering was almost over felt like a warm blanket. But I fell foul of having the wrong expectations. *It's just one more day of riding*, I thought, little appreciating that 'just one more day' meant a full 266 kilometres along tough roads in gale-force winds. I shouldn't have been so casual about what lay ahead. 'Just one more day' can be the biggest day of your life.

There was another welcome visit from the race organisers. A few hours outside Karasjok the white Volkswagen pulled alongside and Andrea leaned out of the window again to deliver perhaps the most ominous sentence I have ever heard.

'Okay, so don't you worry about D––– no more. He is...' and then he slowly drew his thumb across his throat while making a choking noise. It later turned out that this gesture meant 'disqualified', but at the time it just looked deeply troubling and I didn't ask for clarification in case I didn't like the answer. I faced forwards and nodded.

A few minutes later, back on my own after Andrea's car had turned back, I decided that being told not to worry about DR, even by a race official, was not enough for me. Whether DR was disqualified from the race, or merely got a time penalty for shortcutting, I did not want my victory to be in any way tainted. It became incredibly important to me that I would literally be the very first person to reach the finish line, even if DR had taken a shortcut. Indeed, if he had taken a shortcut then it was *especially* important I got to the finish first. DR needed to be left in no doubt that he had been beaten: I wanted no muttering about winning on a technicality; I wanted no 'Yeah, maybe Ian finished first *if you don't count...*'. I'd worked far too hard to deal with that noise. As much as my exhausted body would allow it, I began to dig deeper and push even harder.

It helped that the landscape in those far reaches of Norway was so magical. Reindeer appeared in twos and threes, silently cropping the grass on the low hills to my left. To my right was a wide fjord of unimprovable stillness and beauty. As the shadows of low clouds skimmed across the dark and silent waters, I fell again into that perfect state of oneness with my activity. Entirely absorbed in the flow of riding my bike, I was overcome by a deep sense of peace and control. And that feeling lasted, and lasted. Tears of gratitude welled in my eyes as the ecstasy overtook me. *To think I might have lived without experiencing this*, I thought, watching the ruffled sea gently lap the shore.

Eventually the route turned away from the fjord, leaving behind the scattered red fishing houses and tall racks of fish drying in the pure Arctic winds. With the sea out of sight, the road plummeted into the Nordkapp Tunnel that takes travellers to Magerøya Island: a laser-straight plunge down a steep slope until I was 250 metres below the deep and deadly waters. The tunnel went on for six kilometres, its claustrophobic darkness booming with the reverberations of passing cars. The approach of each car built and built for what seemed like an impossibly long time, the confined space making the noise reach unimaginable levels, as though I was hearing the approach of a vast aircraft rather than a simple domestic car. The sound of each vehicle took on an eerie throbbing quality, growing in volume all the while, but still the car would not appear. Louder and louder still, until it felt the whole world was noise, before finally the car would pass, its booming fading with imperceptible slowness as the tail lights receded into the distance.

In short, that tunnel really put the willies up me.

Back at the surface, after a slow 10% climb out of the up-side-down mountain that was the tunnel, my trials were still not over. I found myself blasted by powerful winds that whipped my front wheel from side to side, almost throwing me to the tarmac several times. It seemed that no matter how close I got to the finish, I still could not find peace. I was not free to enjoy the end of this race; always there was some fresh torment between me and the finish line. The wind built until I was leaning sideways at a bizarre angle just to keep grinding slowly forward. Each passing vehicle blocked the wind for a moment, making me fight to regain control as I started to fall over sideways, only for me to be-gin an equal and opposite fight a second later when the vehicle passed and the blustery wind resumed.

And the hills! Why couldn't this ride just end?! I was only a few kilometres from the finish, but the road went up and down a series of brutal climbs, made all the harder by my deep exhaustion and the ever-present gales. The race or-ganisers' car pulled alongside, and the camera operator leaned out of the window to film me. I was standing on the pedals, hauling on the handlebars, giving it everything I had just to get up those slopes. I climbed 150 metres, then plummeted down to sea level to do it all over again. And then... blessedly... finally, there it was. A sign rolled by read-ing 'Nordkapp 500 m'. Fighting the winds, ignoring the fire in my legs, I fixated on the North Cape visitors' centre, sit-ting ahead of me atop of the very last slope in Europe. Just one more push and I would be there...

'Victory'

When you work in a university psychology department, it is common to get requests to help out with research. A few years ago an email went around our whole department asking for volunteers to take a short survey. Having a few spare minutes, I followed the link.

The questionnaire was revelatory. Some of the items described my secret inner workings so well that I almost suspected it was a hoax. I was asked to rate how much I agreed with statements like 'When I work towards something and it goes well, this is more of a relief than anything else'. *Yes, that's it exactly*, I thought, clicking the top end of the rating scale.

I later learned that this questionnaire was based on an idea called Regulatory Focus Theory. The basic idea is that you can be driven to gain positive outcomes (a *promotion focus*) or you can be driven to avoid something going wrong (a *prevention focus*). Each of us tends to favour one of these two approaches as we work towards a goal. In other words, the same success can mean different things to different people.

How do you tell if you are more of a promotion or a prevention person? Imagine the end of a tennis match, as one player knocks the ball past the other to win. Do they roar and hold their arms aloft, basking in the cheers of the crowd, or do they slump with relief now their ordeal is over without anything having gone wrong along the way? The former person, who feels elation when they achieve a goal and disappointment when they do not, is promotion-focused: their target is to achieve victory. The latter person is prevention-focused: their goal is not to avoid defeat, but to avoid messing up on their path to the win.

And so it was for me at the end of the North Cape 4000.

As I rolled the last few metres to the end of the world and unclipped from the pedals, there was no elation, no joy. All I thought was three short words, echoing around my head over and over as I pushed those last few hundred metres: *it is done.* At last I could stop.

> **It's done**
> **North Cape 4000**
> **4322 km**
> **11 days, 10 hours, 44 minutes**
> **I am humbled by everybody's support**

It was only hours later, slouched in a chair in the visitor centre waiting for the southbound bus and explaining what I had done to curious tourists, that I started to feel like I had really achieved something. But at the same time, there was already a troubling itch at the back of my mind. Once again, I slowly found myself fixing on a clear and startling realisation:

I could have done that faster.

Lessons from North Cape

Looking back on my unexpected first place in the North Cape 4000, and the surprising levels of effort and aggression I found within myself along the way, I decided it was again important to try to extract lessons for the future. Let's start with the specifics.

1. Faffing is the enemy of progress
When I checked my Strava records after the ride, I was surprised to see just how much time I spent not moving. On the best days, I moved for 89 or 90 per cent of the time between starting out in the morning and stopping at night, which is a really good proportion – especially considering that includes the time spent waiting at traffic lights and

suchlike. Day 6, for example, when I rode from Poland into Lithuania, saw me stationary for just 1 hour and 50 minutes out of a 16-hour day (let us politely skip over the fact I stopped after only 16 hours of riding). But while such days were disciplined and solid, other days were dramatically worse. Day 10 – the one that ended with me forced off the road by cold weather – saw me stationary for almost 5 hours out of 18 hours and 35 minutes of riding. That was a terrible statistic. I decided in future I needed to be much more disciplined about this.

2. The common route reduced stress
The requirement for all the North Cape riders to follow exactly the same route meant there was one less thing to worry about. I knew that several minds had checked over this route, reducing the likelihood that last year's Macedonian goat-track debacle would be repeated. Even if it were, the common route meant there was a level playing field for all the competitors and we would all have suffered equally. Every time I found myself on a bad road, or crawling slowly through a city, there was no real worry about this because I knew it was the same for everybody else. Having such a major responsibility taken away was liberating.

3. You cannot be too self-sufficient
Day three of the NC4K saw me having to stop several hours earlier than I would have liked, and in a less-than-ideal mountain-top location, because my lights, computer, phone and battery charger were all low on power. After the race, I decided that I could enjoy more flexibility if I made myself more self-sufficient with a dynamo power and lighting system. I asked Judith Stayer to make me a replacement front wheel with a Son dynamo, and fitted dynamo-powered front and rear lights, plus a USB charging system. This proved revolutionary, and I immediately regretted not having done it sooner. The dynamo-powered headlamp illuminated the road far beyond anything I had used before; to

get that sort of power from even a top-end battery lamp would have drained the battery in less than an hour. But now I could have total illumination right through the night without having to worry about depleting my resources. The light was bright enough that I could descend hills at 50 or 60 kph without concern. And although the dynamo didn't quite kick out enough power to run the headlight and battery charger at the same time, it was not a hardship to charge my phone and bike computer during the day and then discharge them at night.

4. The machine burns a lot of fuel
Speaking of energy demands, a ride like this burns through huge amounts. The sheer quantities of food needed to replace this became a real challenge. A long day of endurance riding can consume an extra 8000 or even 10,000 calories of energy over what you would use sitting still. Finding and consuming that much food is a time-consuming process for the unsupported rider. Petrol stations were the quickest and most convenient source of food, but these often had very limited options, and what was available was usually little more than sugary sweets or unhelpfully fragile pretzel snacks. Supermarkets had more options, including great on-the-go staples like bananas. Latvia's incredible one-kilogramme family pouches of yoghurt were a particular treat. But using a supermarket took a lot of time compared to petrol stations: in each supermarket I had to lose valuable minutes wandering the aisles looking for what I needed, always uncertain if they would even sell what I was looking for. The international nature of the race added a particular challenge here: the brands available in the shops changed every time I crossed a border, so I never knew from one day to the next what products would be available, nor what the packages I needed would look like. Each nation's supermarkets have a maddeningly different system for how they sell fruit and bread. All of this ate a lot more valuable time.

My constant quest for energy was made particularly pressing by the extra pace and effort I needed to get ahead in the race and then stay there. I was surprised to see just how much more physically demanding it was to go from riding fast to riding *as fast as possible*. The diminishing returns of air resistance meant that a small increase in speed needed a huge extra increase in effort. This in turn meant I needed a lot more food than I had on the Transcontinental the previous year. The near-constant consumption of food extracted a price from my body. Towards the end of my ride to North Cape, my tongue became swollen and sore. After days of sugary junk, my stomach lost the taste for anything sweet. Eventually I found I was struggling to eat anything solid at all, and the final stretches of the ride were largely powered by my fail-safe sources of easy-to-swallow energy: milkshakes and yoghurt.

The true lessons from the North Cape 4000

I hope that the practical insights above might be useful if you choose to race yourself. But I think that, again, the more interesting lessons from this experience were deeper and more personal. Thankfully, I wrote some notes soon after finishing the NC4K. This means I can share with you the thoughts that were fresh in my mind when I returned home from the race.

1. It's nice to know you have definitely, unambiguously done a good job
For many people in today's information age, the nebulous and ill-defined nature of our jobs means we are never really sure when we have finished our work. 'Work' today is often a thousand overlapping micro-tasks with no clear picture of how they fit together or what is the end goal. And just as we are unable to know when we have finished our labour, nor are we sure when we have done a good job. What does truly

great office work even look like? What is the ideal towards which we are striving? What a delight it was to undertake a task where all the boundaries were agreed in advance, where the finish was entirely clear and I could know exactly the extent to which I had done a good job. Racing North Cape 4000 was a delicious break from ambiguity.

2. You can only control the process, not the outcome
On an event of this scale, the only thing you can control is what you are doing *right now*. You cannot control the outcome of the race, because this would mean controlling the weather, the traffic and, above all, the actions of your competitors. There is nothing you can do about these variables, and so the only healthy option is to abandon all attempts to influence them. At any given time on the NC4K, the only things I could control where what I was doing right then: I could eat if I needed food, drink if I needed water, speed up if I was riding too easy or slow down if I was riding too hard. These micro-actions were all that I could control, and I learned how vital it was that I attended to them closely. I had to influence only what I could influence and trust that this was all I could do to make the right outcome more likely.

Later, I reflected on how this is another example where ultradistance sport provides a great metaphor for life. Few of us can take any action today that definitively shapes our future. If we have a long-term goal – career success, becoming fit, maintaining a long and happy relationship with a loved one – then there is nothing we can do today to make sure that happens. All we can do is control what is controllable in the short term. You can't do anything today to ensure your partner is still happy with you in 20 years, but you can certainly try to make sure they are happy with you *now*.[5] It is then just a question of attending to that small daily task for the next 20 years. Eventual success is the ac-

5 I am not claiming to be great at this one in practice. Sport is definitely easier.

cumulation of a thousand tiny actions, and all any of us can do is ask: what is the right action *right now?*

3. *There is a deep satisfaction from undertaking something difficult*

Our everyday lives might be frustrating, ambiguous, or complex. But they are rarely outright *difficult*. They do not demand that we strip back to the basic essentials of existence. As such, it can be rewarding to step away for a time and engage in something that is both very simple and very hard. There is a joy and a liberation in being stripped back to the basics of existence – food, water, shelter, movement. Doing this means you are able to devote the entirety of your mind – indeed, the entirety of your existence – to completing a series of simple, actionable tasks. This focus on specifics, this concretisation of life, proved for me to be deeply rewarding. As in my earlier rides, I couldn't tell you what I thought about as I rode to North Cape. I was too mentally absorbed in the simple but pressing demands of meeting my basic needs ever to be bored.

4. *Winners are treated differently*

I've never won anything before, and certainly not a relatively high-profile international race. Goodness me, what attention you get! When I finished the Transcontinental the previous year – at that time, the hardest thing I had done – I got congratulatory messages from friends and family, of course, and plenty of nice messages from people I knew online. But what a difference when I finished a race in first place! Suddenly my feats were being reported on Global Cycling Network's racing news; I was getting showered with emails from people I didn't previously know; offers of free equipment; invites to do media interviews and public talks; people from all around the globe suddenly following me on Strava. The world really does love a winner. I can see how people find it addictive.

5. You can always do just a little bit more
There were, inarguably, times on the way to North Cape that were deeply challenging. There were moments when I felt fatigued beyond belief, and times where thoughts of the task ahead threatened to overwhelm me. In these moments, I was saved from despair by my ultradistance experience. No matter how bad things got, I reassured myself that I could always turn the pedals one more time, I could always reach that next tree, I could always get to the end of this road... Breaking down the enormity of my task into small chunks never failed to keep me moving. Who, after all, cannot turn the pedal just one more time?

6. We are defined by our choices
In the aftermath of the North Cape 4000, I slowly was forced to realise that finishing first was not an accident. It was the product of choices, and I could very easily have made different choices and lost out on what I achieved. I chose to push hard through Latvia and Estonia when I spotted a chance to get ahead. I then chose to push even harder for the following 1600 kilometres to maintain and grow my lead over the rest of the pack, and I chose to endure the mental and physical suffering that this involved. And these choices were only made possible by other choices: I made the choice to focus on the process of riding rather than the goal, and for months beforehand I had made the choice to train hard – without which none of these other things would have been possible. I chose to enter a race I knew would be difficult, and I chose to fight once I was in it. All these things were within my choosing and the eventual success arose from making a long sequence of good choices and following through with them.

Part 4
Going Further

I could have done that faster. The thought was still with me some weeks after returning from North Cape, and so I started to think about how I might build upon my success in the following year. I settled on another attempt at the Transcontinental Race. Off the back of NC4K, it felt fitting to go back and ride against the very top people in the sport again. A part of me – the tedious imposter syndrome part – was worrying that finishing first at North Cape had been some sort of fluke. That same self-doubting part of me assumed that most observers would be thinking the same thing. Going up against the very best riders seemed like a way perhaps to set my mind at rest.

And then, as if from nowhere, a new idea settled into my head and made itself at home. Looking back, I have no idea what started this, but I was suddenly seized with the notion of attempting to break an ultradistance world record rather than enter a race. It felt like the more attractive way to use the skills that I had discovered on the way to North Cape. I think what appealed to me most was the elegant simplicity of the thing. There would be no staring at my phone worrying about other competitors and their unpredictable journeys: it would be just me against the clock. A race of truth. And also a race spread across time, in which anybody could compete against anybody else at a moment of their own choosing. I would be racing the last person to break the record, and if I was successful, the next person to come along would be racing us both. A race like this could, in theory, unfold over centuries.

I was aware of Sean Conway's record-breaking solo ride from Portugal to Russia about a year earlier, as it had received quite a lot of attention at the time. I also knew that Sean's trans-European record had recently been beaten by Leigh Timmis, who had ridden a more northerly route between the start and end points and who had used a support crew, unlike Sean who had travelled alone. (Guinness Records don't distinguish between supported and unsupported rides, and don't make stipulations about the route, so these two riders competed for the same record even though they did it in very different ways.) Leigh had sent me an email shortly after I returned from NC4K, telling me about his plans and suggesting we have a chat to see if I had any insights to pass on. Unfortunately he started his ride soon after getting in touch and we didn't find a chance to talk. Somehow, despite not hearing my confused and disconnected thoughts on endurance racing, Leigh nevertheless averaged an impressive 370 kilometres per day over his 6071-kilometre route between Cabo da Roca and Ufa, handily smashing Sean Conway's record.

It was Leigh's average of 370 kilometres per day that I found myself thinking about a few months later. By this point I had collated all my NC4K data and had seen that, although the distance I travelled had varied a lot from one day to the next, I had averaged 360.2 kilometres per day. I decided that if I trained with a focus on getting faster and spending less time stationary, I should easily be capable in future of pushing that up and averaging – what? – 400 kilometres each day? I didn't know if I would then be able to maintain that sort of daily average for 6000 kilometres rather than 4000 kilometres, as that big jump in distance was sure to be a lot more demanding, but once my mind landed on this value of 400 kilometres per day the record seemed like it might just be within my reach. It would be difficult, obviously, but what a challenge! I bought a huge laminated map of Europe and started tracing lines on it with a dry-wipe pen, thinking about possible routes, torn between the manifold potential options. There are, it turns out, an awful lot of ways to cross a continent like Europe with its dense network of roads built over millennia.

One place where there were very few options, however, was Russia. The city of Ufa, at the foot of the Ural mountains, was the official end point for this ride (or start point, if I decided to go east to west – something that tempted me at the time). Whichever route I looked at, it was clear there was no way between Ufa and the European Union without riding at least 2000 kilometres in Russia. It was not the distance that worried me: I was concerned by Russia's lack of road options. There are no secondary roads between towns: it was either major highways or dirt tracks, with nothing in between. Searching for information, I was alarmed by other riders' reports of how dangerous it was to share the highways with an apparently ceaseless procession of speeding trucks. People seemed to be talking about far too many near-death experiences for my liking. But if anything the back roads sounded even more impassable. Plus, there were bears out on those dirt roads.

Ah well, I thought, *the faster I ride the sooner it'll be over.* But I was fooling nobody. I was really scared.

Holly

'I want to give this everything I can possibly give,' I said to Louise. 'I'm 44 and I'm not getting any younger. I want to know, definitively, what my body and mind are capable of. I don't want to look back in the future and wonder if I could have done better if only I'd made a different choice somewhere, or known something extra. I need to give this attempt absolutely everything I can give it so there can be zero regrets twenty years from now.'

'Are you going to get a coach?'

'I'm going to get a coach.'

I met Holly Seear in a cafe in Reading a couple of weeks later. At once, I could tell she was somebody who understood this. She was an experienced competitive rider and held a broad range of the highest cycle coaching qualifications anybody can have. But what really convinced me that she was the right person for the job was her reaction when I raised the idea of a record attempt.

Initially, when Holly asked what my plans were for the coming year, I had said something vague about wanting to build on my NC4K experience and how I was tempted by another shot at the Transcontinental Race. All the time we spoke, I worried she was quietly disapproving of the cake I was eating in the cafe. Eventually, towards the end of our meeting, I decided to float the impossible idea that I had admitted to nobody other than Louise at that point.

'There is one other idea I've had,' I said tentatively. '...What do you think about trying to break a world record?'

Holly's face broke into a huge grin. Yep, this was the right coach.

The ninety-degree turn

A few weeks later, I was looking over the Guinness World Record website to check the details of how to go about officially challenging the record. As I read, I stumbled upon something very intriguing. It turned out there are two records for riding across Europe: the Portugal-Russia route taken by Sean Conway and Leigh Timmis, and a North-South route between North Cape in Norway and Tarifa in Spain – the northernmost and southernmost points on the continent. I raised an eyebrow when I saw that the record for this second route seemed much more achievable: the distance would only be around 300 kilometres longer than the east-west route that Leigh had recently taken, but the current record was around five days slower than his ride had been. It was held by a rider called Lee Fancourt who, I learned from Guinness, had completed the route in 21 days, 14 hours and 23 minutes. *Hmm*, I thought.

I was also attracted to this north-south route by its logic. The west-east route started from Cabo da Roca in Portugal, which is the point of the Eurasian landmass that reaches farthest into the Atlantic. There could be no better western end for this ride. But the other end of the route felt more arbitrary: the Russian city of Ufa sat near the foot of the Ural mountains, but lacked the satisfying geographical perfection of Cabo da Roca. It was *an* easternmost point, but it was not inarguably *the* easternmost point. Why not end in Perm, or Yekaterinburg, or Sterlitamak – or any of the other cities within the Urals? Switching to the north-south route would remove this uncertainty. The route went from what was clearly the northernmost point in Europe to what was clearly the Southernmost. The whole thing just felt more satisfying when I looked at it on a map.

Finally, I was drawn to this new route because it would involve a lot less of the Russian highways that so intimidated me. Guinness record rules stipulated that the ride had to be entirely overland – there could be no ferry like on the North Cape 4000 – and this meant some riding in Russia was going to be inevitable. But I reckoned I could get this down to a few hundred kilometres rather than two thousand or more. This discovery, combined with the apparently less demanding record, confirmed my change of plans. I was going to ride North-South instead.

Holly didn't have any space in her schedule to start coaching me until mid-November, but when she did become available it was interesting to see what she prescribed. I had explained that I was always going to cycle to and from work, and so there was no option but to use these commutes as the backbone of my training. Although this wasn't what she was used to, Holly rose to the challenge and began to fill my diary with instructions about exactly how I was to do these rides. The main thing she got me to do was slow down. Under her tuition, my typical commute became both simple and sedate: I was to ride the 41 kilometres between home and work without my heart rate ever going above 130 – in other words, I was not to push myself hard at all. Many days I did this in both directions, for a total of 82 kilometres of plodding. It felt slow, especially as my route is quite hilly, with around 900 metres climbing for the round trip. But thankfully there was far more to my training regime than these long slow rides, and on other days I was given instructions on specific workouts using hard intervals at specific power levels. I was also made to take more rest days than I might otherwise have taken. I started to feel the benefit within weeks.

Holly was great at making me think about aspects of my riding that I had previously skipped over. Before a long ride, she had me work out exactly what the energy requirements were likely to be, and what I would need to eat to fuel this effort. I was surprised, when I calculated it all properly rather than rely on guesswork, to see that I needed considerably more food than I would normally have guessed. After these rides were complete, Holly had me reflect on them. What had gone well? What could I have done differently? It was good to be forced to think about these things that I would more naturally have ignored.

Perhaps one of the best bits of being coached was having somebody else to look after both the large-scale and small-scale planning. Holly thought through the whole of the next few months to devise an overarching scheme that would see me at peak fitness the following June. She then broke this down to specific once- or twice-daily workouts that told me exactly how to ride and for how long. At first I was apprehensive about this process, but I quickly realised this arrangement was not going to work unless I trusted my coach. I made an explicit choice to believe everything she said. Soon I grew to love the freedom that came from this surrender, from having somebody else do so much of my thinking for me. I liked turning on my bicycle computer

ENDLESS PERFECT CIRCLES   119

each morning and seeing the instructions for that day's ride pop up automatically. Once I made that decision to place my training entirely in Holly's hands, no longer did I have to fight the nagging doubt that I might be using each day more productively.

It was a leap of faith. It paid off.

Together with Holly, I also started to work out the riding strategy I would use for the record attempt. Around this time I read Mark Beaumont's book about breaking the world record for cycling around the world and became intrigued by his approach of riding in four-hour blocks, each of which was followed by a thirty-minute rest. I decided to experiment with doing something similar. Obviously I lacked Mark Beaumont's extensive support crew and resources. As soon as four hours' riding had elapsed, he had been able to climb into a vehicle containing a bed, a physiotherapist and stacks of nutritious food. I, in my unsupported version of his approach, had to clump around a petrol station buying cakes and ice creams and then eat these while standing on the concrete of the forecourt and rubbing my calf muscles against a bollard. But, for all I lacked his resources, his method translated to unsupported riding quite well. Four hours' riding is, give or take, 100 kilometres. So I would look for shops or petrol stations 100 kilometres apart and use these as my rest stops. The exact locations of these facilities was outside my control, so sometimes this meant I had to stop after three hours or push on for an extra hour or more, and this wasn't ideal, but having clear blocks of time to work with nevertheless proved a useful strategy. I was able to sail past enticing shops, comfortable in the knowledge that I had a plan that allowed me to keep on moving without fear I would not be able to resupply. It was all pre-arranged, and this was liberating.

I also found that this approach meant I was free to take proper rest breaks. In the past, my food stops had always been as short as possible: I would cram something down my throat and get right back on the bike, always aware of the ticking clock or the approaching competitor. When I started experimenting with the strategy of four hour blocks, and taking a full 30 minutes of rest after each, it felt like luxury. I was able to sit down and eat; I could stretch my muscles and really relax, comfortable in the knowledge that this was all part of the plan. Because I had set out in the morning with the intention of resting for 30 minutes after each block of riding, I was freed from the usual nagging urgency to get back on the bike and be moving again without delay. It was all part of the plan. Trust the plan.

Most important of all, this approach broke my long rides into manageable portions. This was critical if my mind was not to be overwhelmed by the enormity of what I was doing. Every ultradistance athlete quickly learns that it is essential to break down the task ahead into manageable chunks. Often, when the going gets hard, this might take the form of coaxing yourself along with thoughts like 'It's 10 k to the next stop – that's the distance from home to that nice cafe I sometimes visit. I've done that loads of times, so I know I can do it now.' For this record attempt, I started working with a large-scale version of this same strategy. From all my past riding, I knew with deep certainty that I could definitely ride 100 kilometres. That's something I'd do in a morning without really thinking about it. *And if I know I can ride 100k*, I thought, *it's just a question of doing that more than once.* The idea of riding 6300 kilometres was unimaginable, but the idea of riding 100 kilometres sixty-three times felt... well, if not easy, then at least conceivable.

One reason this sort of mental strategy was so necessary for the record attempt was that my planned daily distance was exactly the distance most feared by audax riders. Audax events usually fall into one of five main distances: 200, 300, 400, 600 and 1000 kilometres, and it is the 400 that leads to the most nervous muttering. This is because 200 or 300 kilometres is basically a long day's riding – you start in the morning and finish in the evening, and although it will obviously be more demanding than a typical day on the bike, it is still fundamentally business as usual to an audax rider. A 600- or 1000-kilometre trip is a massive undertaking, but the difficulty is softened somewhat by the ride being spread across two or even three days, with a break for a short sleep. Indeed, in the case of a Thousand, riders are likely to have two short sleeps. But a 400-kilometre ride is right in the middle of the range: it is too long simply to be a big day ride, but it is not long enough to justify a sleep stop. With its awkward time limit of 27 hours, many people find the 400 to be the most gruelling and demanding of distances, yet this is what I had chosen to be the daily staple of my record attempt. Moreover, I was going to have to complete each day's riding in far less than 27 hours if I wanted more than – 3 hours of sleep per night.

It was around this time that I began to learn more about Lee Fancourt, whose trans-European record I was challenging. It was not a happy story. Had I been involved in ultra-cycling a few years earlier, I would probably have known it already, as Lee had been quite well known in the field. In 2012 he had ridden around the world in a little over 103 days – an attempt that probably broke the record for the fastest circumnavigation of the planet at the time, but which was never officially ratified because he deviated from his journey to help his support crew when they ran into some difficulty and did not return to the exact point where he had left the route. He did, however, manage to clock a series of other official Guinness records including the fastest crossing of Europe and several records for covering big distances on a mountain bike.

Lee killed himself in 2018, after struggling with depression. Accounts say that he found life difficult whenever he was off his bike, only being at ease when riding. Learning his story added a bitter taste to what I was doing, and for a long time I wondered if it was even appropriate for me to try to take the record in such circumstances. Should it, I wondered, be left to stand in perpetuity as a form of memorial?

Rivals

I race so I can train; I don't train so I can race.

The idea that I might enjoy the occasional spurt of racing but resent all the preparation for it is ridiculous to me. Why would I put myself through that? If I did not enjoy the training, none of this would happen. Racing is the price I pay for the fun of training.

Under Holly's supervision, I continued to train hard and regularly. Eighteen or twenty hours' riding in a week was typical, and often I did more than this when I undertook long weekend rides on top of my commutes. I rode through sun, I rode through rain and, above all, I rode through wind – thousands of kilometres of it. I rode when I was in the mood to do it and I rode when I was not in the mood to do it.

Sticking so tightly to my training schedule was made easier by a bit of psychology that, coincidentally, I spend a lot of time investigating in my day job: habit. I have done research on habits with my lovely colleague Bas Verplanken since around 2007. Like a lot of psychological terms, 'habit' is an everyday word that has been co-opted into science. (This is inevitable in psychology, since psychologists are often interested in trying to explain everyday experiences.) To be a bit more specific, for researchers like Bas and I, a habit is a behaviour that is triggered by your circumstances without your really having to think about it. Although you might start out carefully considering any given action that you take, once you have repeated it over and over at the same time or in the same place, you might find yourself do-ing it without much thought because that action is now triggered more or less automatically by that particular time or that particular place. When you go to bed, for example, I suspect you might find yourself in the bathroom brushing your teeth without really having given it very much thought. The activity is so tightly tied into your daily routine that, when the time comes to go to bed, a largely unconscious process tells you to go to the bathroom and start your ablutions without having to bother your conscious self all that much.

Habits usually take a long time to form, but once they exist, they linger and can be tough to get rid of – it is literally true that old habits die hard, and I carried out the study that first showed this. A real-life example of how difficult it can be to overcome habits arose while I was writing this book. My local council announced they were going to close one of the roads I commute along for a week, so that they could carry out some repairs. I knew this in advance, and the night before the road closure began I even checked a map to plan an alternative route. Yet what did I do the next morning? I autopiloted all the way to the closed road and only remembered all my careful planning when I got there. That is the power of habit.

But habit can also be a positive thing. And this is what I found when I built my training into my regular commute. Slipping into cycling kit and getting on the bike most mornings became a part of my life that did not require much thought – it just happened, because that was what I did. Although an occasional ride could be unpleasant if the weather was bad, I never really thought about not doing it. After a while, it felt like more trouble *not* to cycle to work than it was to ride the bike – and that is as useful a measure of habit as you'll find.

And thus Winter slowly gave way to Spring. And when it did, I learned that I was not the only person to notice that Lee Fancourt's record was ripe for breaking.

First I discovered that a British rider called Ryan Anderton was planning an attempt, and shortly afterwards I discovered yet another local, Rob Gardiner, was doing the same thing. I learned about both through word of mouth within the cycling community, and the discoveries threw me. Rival riders going for the same record could ruin everything, especially if one of them made their attempt before me and set a record I very obviously could not beat.

What would it feel like to set off from North Cape with that looming over me? Would it even be worth making my attempt? But if one of these other riders smashed the record beyond my ability and I called off my ride as a lost cause, what about the money I had already spent on coaching and flights? What about all the training I had done? What about all the people with whom I had shared my plans? You might imagine how these thoughts did not contribute to restful sleep.

I began stalking Rob and Ryan on Strava, to see what sort of distances and speeds they seemed capable of. I also made contact with them, to tell them what I was planning and to get our 'rivalries' out in the open. Quite soon the order of events became clear: Rob was going to make his attempt four weeks before me and Ryan was going to set off shortly after I was due to finish. My research suggested that both riders were strong, but I saw that both of them had relatively little experience of ultradistance riding – and, especially, neither of them had done any ultradistance *racing*. It is one thing to ride 350 kilometres in a day, but quite another to do it as fast as you can manage and then get up and do it all again the next day, and the next, and the next... Until you have been there, you cannot entirely know what that is like. Once I saw their lack of racing experience, both riders continued to worry me, but perhaps not quite to the same degree. I started to sleep a little easier.

The greater blow to morale came when I got a message from two-time Transcontinental winner James Hayden telling me that he was going to make his own attempt on this same record. James, you might recall, was waiting at the finish line when I got to the end of the TCR having finished more than three days ahead of me.

He won't know this, but if James's goal had been to demoralise his rival, he could not have picked a psychologically more damaging time to break the news to me about his record ambitions. I was in my shed, entirely failing to get a new tubeless tyre onto my rear wheel rim. My thumbs were both blistered from trying to force the tyre into place, and my arms ached from thirty minutes of fruitless wrestling and squeezing. Struggling with this most simple bit of maintenance meant I was having all sorts of terrible visions about what might go wrong on a Russian roadside if I could not even manage this in my own home. It was at this peak of self-doubt that my phone buzzed and James's message popped into view:

> "Hi Ian, hope you're well. Good to see you're going for N-T record. In confidence, I'm doing the same this year. But in mid August, so it won't impact your attempt. Pretty cool there are 4 people including us both going for it!"

This was a problem. James was easily one of the best long-distance cyclists on the planet. He didn't just have unusual physical strength – although he possessed that in spades – he also had the full range of talents that ultradistance riding requires: mental fortitude, route-planning, problem-solving. You don't win the Transcontinental Race twice by accident.

To my surprise, though, after just a few days I found I had gone from being alarmed and disheartened by this new development to making peace with it. As James suggested, it helped a lot that he was planning to ride after me. I would be able to make my best attempt on the record and if he came along afterwards and took it from me, then so be it. I would, at least, be able to say I had broken a world record – that was enough for me. And despite James's physical strength, 6300 kilometres is still a hell of a long ride. A lot can happen over that sort of distance; there was no guarantee that the rider with the greatest raw power would finish fastest. I learned that when I managed to get ahead of the obviously stronger Paolo Botti during the North Cape 4000.

Learn to enjoy the suffering

Much as these friendly rivalries occupied my mind, the period leading up to the record attempt saw me more concerned with training. I continued my regular bicycle commutes, and Holly started increasingly to give me longer weekend training rides. These often included a session I came to dread: three or four hours of steady riding followed by a series of 15-minute hill-climbs at threshold pace. Immediately as the last of these climbs ended, I was instructed to go into five minutes of flat-out riding, leaving nothing in the tank. That session invariably ended with me collapsed by the side of the road, swearing feebly at the distant black birds that floated above me so effortlessly in the grey Mendip skies.

But my preparations were not all this disciplined, and the months between finishing North Cape 4000 and starting the record attempt were filled with several rides of memorable idiocy. In August, just three weeks after the NC4K ended, I caught up with Richard Coomer – whom I first met on the Pennine 600 – to ride the Mille Cymru audax: one thousand hilly kilometres on a glorious route that zig-zagged across Wales. Perhaps my overarching memory of our weekend was when Richard and I sat eating outside a fish-and-chip shop in Bala early one evening after a tough day of climbing. A bird did a massive shit over my dinner and I was so hungry that I just pushed the shit to one side and carried on eating, almost without pause.

A couple of months later, in December, I came back for an even tougher trip to Wales after champion 24-hour mountain biker Matt Jones organised a charity ride around the entire coastline of Britain. Matt's vision was to raise money and awareness for mental health charities by having ten riders undertake a twenty-day relay around the very edge of Britain in Winter. Inspired by the mental health theme, the ride was deliberately timed to end on 21 December: the darkest day of the year. After being introduced through a chance meeting with a Bristol-based rider called Alan Colville, Matt asked me to undertake the first leg of the ride: a 735-kilometre stretch that started in Bristol and went around much of the Welsh coast. I had a strict deadline of exactly 48 hours before I had to hand over to the next rider in Criccieth. With a total of 8000 metres climbing, all of it up and down savage coastal roads, this was never going to be easy. Undertaking the ride in Winter made it all the harder.

A member of my local cycling club, Robert Wragge-Morley, offered to support my leg of the ride. He perhaps didn't realise that his kind gesture would mean he had to endure a manic two days of driving around increasingly tiny Welsh lanes, jumping out of the support car at irregular intervals to hand me milkshakes, Allen keys and pizzas. The venture was made all the more interesting by the series of intense storms that overwhelmed us almost as soon as Robert and I crossed the Bristol Channel. Now, from the comfort of my warm house a year later, those two days on the *Lap of my Mind* ride come back to me as a series of grim flashbacks: Robert's concerned face as I shivered in a late-night pizza takeaway in Swansea while the locals partied through the rain outside; crawling up a coastal road of such appalling steepness that I had once struggled to ascend it in a car; Robert getting trapped by flooded roads; me crashing hard outside Port Talbot when the cyclepath ended abruptly and scattered me across wet tarmac, shredding my waterproof jacket in the process.

It was all great practice in learning how to enjoy the suffering.

In the Spring of 2019 I started to do big back-to-back rides to test all the various components of my race strategy. One thing I deliberately worked on was making sure I was entirely comfortable with night riding. Riding in the dark initially scares most people. There is a strange feeling of normality being disrupted when you are out alone at night – everything is at once familiar yet somehow wrong, and it is easy to feel vulnerable. But with experience, I came to love these hours of stillness and peace. Having normality disrupted is not such a bad thing given that normality usually involves mixing with swarms of badly driven motor vehicles. There is also an illicit thrill to the whole thing. To ride through a town or village at three in the morning, when everybody else is asleep, can't help but make you think of the possibilities open to you. *I could do anything right now*, you think, and although you might not abuse this power, the knowledge that you have it brings a frisson of excitement.

I practised my overnight riding by setting off from Bristol at sunset and riding 400 kilometres through the darkness to my father's house in Yorkshire. I then did the same the next evening, riding 400 kilometres home through the following night along a different route. Unfortunately, at 0200 that morning, when I was somewhere near Ironbridge, the clocks went forward and my bicycle computer shit the bed, totally unable to account for the sudden jump in time. I couldn't believe the programmers hadn't anticipated this – I'd ridden across time zones before and the computer had managed fine, so I assumed the people who created it would have thought about the clocks changing, given this happens *every single year at an exact pre-planned date and time*. But no. My computer informed me I was travelling backwards at the speed of light before freezing up and wiping a load of valuable riding data. This should, with hindsight, have been a warning of how badly this same computer would let me down on the coming record attempt.

Then the really big shakedown came at Easter weekend. I knew from that earlier overnight ride that my father's house was exactly 400 kilometres from mine, and coincidentally I knew from another back-to-back weekend – one aborted after 180 kilometres thanks to unexpected deep snow – that Norwich was also exactly 400 kilometres from home. *It would be incredibly convenient*, I thought, *if it was also 400 kilometres from my dad's house to Norwich*. And it was, almost to the kilometre. This meant my Easter Triangle ride became a reality: Bristol to Yorkshire to Norwich to Bristol. Loaded down with full race kit, I set out at the start of Good Friday and followed the race strategy exactly. Each day involved four blocks of riding, each as close to 100 kilometres as I could get it, with a proper 30-minute break between each block. Yes, I was pretty weary towards the end, probably because I didn't eat quite enough on the last day, but the ride went really well, and I did the 1200-kilometre triangle at a satisfying average speed of 27 kph.

The very last preparatory ride was a race called All Points North: a wonderfully fun contest in which a load of riders set out from Sheffield on a Friday evening and then tried to get back there as quickly as possible having visited nine checkpoints scattered right across the north of England. We were each free to choose our own route, with the understanding that the shortest possible journey would be almost 900 kilometres (I secretly applied science to the process, working out my route using a travelling salesman algorithm). I did not ride All Points North to win: I was there for a final chance to practice my record-attempt pacing strategy. Accordingly, I rode my route at an intensity that I should have been able to maintain indefinitely, to try to get used to how that level of effort felt over a substantial period of time, and took the same deliberately long breaks that I would take on the record attempt. Despite riding at this relatively easy pace, as though I had set out for a fortnight rather than a weekend, I finished All Points North in fourth place, only about 90 minutes behind the winner and still feeling quite fresh. I counted myself ready to ride.

The outstanding level of fitness I had built from my riding, which peaked at about this time, was a strange thing to experience as somebody who had spent most of his life believing he had no sporting ability. The past two years, particularly since TCR, I had been riding around 25,000 kilometres annually – a greater distance than most people would drive – and for the best part of this time I had been quite deliberately focusing my training with specific workouts. This all meant that I moved beyond merely being fit and into a whole new level of elite physical ability that I had not even glimpsed a few years earlier, and which I still find strange to experience. It was like going from doing a fitness class at a gym twice a week – and being really quite fit as a result – to suddenly being the instructor, who does that same class five times every day. It is not so much stepping up a gear as fitting a whole new engine – one which you hadn't even realised was available. Reaching this elite level of fitness was revelatory.

Waiting for the start

The run-up to the record attempt saw me troubled by doubts of one sort or another. Perhaps most striking, I found that even nine months after the North Cape 4000 had finished, I still regularly had stress dreams as a result of spending all those days being chased by the rest of the pack during my thousand-mile breakaway. Perhaps once a fortnight I would wake from a dream where I was under immense pressure to ride my bike but, for one reason or another, was entirely unable to make any progress. Sometimes the problem would be that I had a series of mechanical breakdowns; more often I dreamt I was preoccupied with trivial tasks like packing and repacking my luggage bags and would then discover that everybody else in the race had left me behind while I faffed around. I started to question whether the drive to compete at such a high level was putting me under pressure that I was not entirely suited for.

I was also troubled by thoughts of the danger. Ultradistance cycling is a very safe activity except for the fact we do it on roads that are shared with motorists, too many of whom are not up to the task and who are not held particularly accountable for the harm they cause. In 2017, the year I rode the Transcontinental Race, the ultracycling world saw a handful of high-profile deaths. Eric Fishbein was killed during the Transamerica Bike Race, and Frank Simons was killed by a motorist on the first day of the Transcontinental Race. At the start of the year, Mike Hall, the founder of the Transcontinental, was killed by a driver while he raced across Australia. Mike's death hit me hard from a distance. I had been eager to meet him in Meteora so I could thank him for all that his race had inspired in me. And now, thanks to one sub-standard Australian motorist and a criminal justice system that did not take road death seriously, I would never get that chance.

Of course, I know the statistics. I know them better than almost anybody: cycle safety is a big part of my professional work. I know that, although these three riders were killed, thousands of other riders rode the same distances on the same roads without incident. And I know that taking part in a race is not really any different from spending the same amount of time riding my bike back at home. Most importantly, I know that my life expectancy goes up rather than down if I ride my bike, since I am far more likely to be killed by a disease linked to inactivity if I don't cycle than I am to be killed by a motorist if I do. But, critically, there is a gulf between these objective facts and my subjective experience, in which near-misses from inattentive and aggressive motorists happen far too often. To put this all another way: cycling a long way on the road is really quite safe, but it doesn't always feel like it. And so, from time to time, I found myself falling into a strangely fatalistic state of mind as I contemplated the ride ahead of me. I pictured a near future in which I was no longer around, and found myself curiously at ease with the thought. It proved particularly convenient for procrastinating at work: *I could write that grant proposal*, I would think, *but that would be a sad waste of effort if I went and got killed before the reviews came back. Let's do something more fun instead.*

But these morbid moments were only infrequent, and I wouldn't want to give the impression I spent months wrapped in fear. Mostly I was worried about the process of racing rather than whatever risks existed, and whether I would be capable of completing the daunting challenge I had set myself. The last month before the record attempt was particularly difficult, as I waited impatiently for the start. With three weeks to go, an email from my coach Holly forced me to face the truth that every athlete knows but does not want to acknowledge: "You're not going to get any fitter at this point," she reminded me. Time hung heavy around my neck – always I was aware of something huge and shapeless looming ahead, pulling my attention unhelpfully from my daily life. And there was nothing to be done. It wasn't like waiting for a party or some other big event, when there is always some task or other; there was nothing I could usefully prepare, because everything was already complete. All I could do was mark time. Perhaps waiting for the arrival of your firstborn is something like this, but I've not had children so wouldn't know. Lacking that comparison, all I could think it that it was like waiting for an execution. If I could have brought forward the start date I would have done it in an instant.

I wanted to hasten the start not least because I found the attention difficult. For the past two years I had used my big rides as a way to raise money and awareness for a wonderful road safety charity called Roadpeace, and I was doing the same again this year. Because there was a charity that was going to benefit from my efforts, it was important to tell people what I was doing. But at the same time, I felt uncomfortable because to talk about such big plans felt like bragging about something I wanted to do but had not yet accomplished. Weighed down by my prevention-focus mindset, I would have been a lot more comfortable crowing about something I had already achieved than something I might yet fail.

Finally, those last couple of weeks also saw me worrying about illness. All it would take is picking up an infection to hinder the start of the ride. I washed my hands repeatedly, and simply avoided human beings as much as possible. But in the end it was all for nothing: some friends visited on my last weekend at home and their two-year-old child got me good. I headed off to Norway with a dribbling nose and elevated heart rate.

Part 5
Crossing Europe

'I never thought I'd be back here again, and yet here I am at the end of the world...'

I was recording a short video on my phone, standing in the blustery wind outside the entrance of the North Cape visitor centre. This deep doorway of stone and wood was one of the two official end points of the route between North Cape and Tarifa. The other was a causeway that jutted into the sea at the southernmost tip of Spain. Standing there at North Cape, shivering with cold and buffeted by gales, Spain seemed unimaginably distant. It was as though I were setting out to cycle to Neptune rather than the other end of Europe. The only way to handle such enormity was not to think about it and to focus instead on the short stretch immediately ahead of me. *Let's just get to the end of this road and see what happens then.* This coping strategy would prove essential over the coming weeks.

The need to focus on the task ahead of me was especially acute, because Rob Gardiner had broken the record just a few days earlier. Rob took over two days off the previous record time with an average daily distance of around 325 kilometres, or 200 miles. I now had only 19 days and 11 hours to get this job done, my margin of comfort significantly reduced.

It was 21 June, yet my hands were chilled and clumsy after removing my gloves to operate the phone a few moments earlier. Nevertheless, I was thrilled to be back. My long journey up had been a series of worries: would my bike make it through two flights without damage? Would I be able to find the bus from Alta – the northernmost airport in Norway – to North Cape? Would I arrive to find I had forgotten to pack some small but vital component like my saddle or my pedals? Would I be able to get my bike on the bus? I was unaccountably relieved to have made it through all of these steps without any problems. I was so delighted to be there on time with all my kit that I almost didn't mind discovering that the bus driver had overcharged me for the trip.

I completed the short video announcing my departure and sent it up to Twitter, where it at once received several thousand views. Clearly I was not going to be alone on this trip – there were quite a few dotwatchers out there who would be following me. Their presence was both a comfort and a concern. There was no backing out now.

I stamped my feet and jumped up and down for warmth as I watched the clock on my cycle computer count up to midday on Midsummer's day – the poetic time I had chosen to begin my venture. I had travelled to North Cape alone, so nobody was watching as I climbed onto the bike at exactly 1200, pressed START on my computer and began to pedal down the gentle slope in front of the visitors' centre. It was a typically low-key beginning for a big event in the toughest sport that nobody has heard of.

Finnmark

It was a joy finally to be underway. As soon as I found myself in the saddle, my hands resting on fresh handlebar tape and my feet beginning to turn in their familiar perfect circles, I felt a weight rise from my back which I had not fully realised was there. For months, my life had been focused on this event. My mental resources had been dedicated to getting me here without anything going wrong. Now that I was at last underway, all my worries were suddenly replaced by a deep sense of purpose. All the questions were suddenly answered. *This is who I am*, I knew. *This is what I do.*

As the road dropped down the coast and hugged the edge of the steep brown cliffs, my bike rolled true beneath me. Its lines and curves were like familiar extensions of my own body, its behaviour predictable and reassuring. The new tyres hummed audibly over the smooth Norwegian road as if they too were pleased to be underway at last.

Forewarned by last year's experience, I was less intimidated by the North Cape Tunnel. It helped that this was the beginning of the journey, meaning I was fresh and fired with enthusiasm rather than exhausted and emotional. My power meter started playing up a bit, and I had to stop a couple of times to jiggle its batteries, but other than this the first leg of my trip could not have been smoother. After the tunnel, I picked up a nice tailwind from the north that helped push me the 249 kilometres back to Alta at an average speed of 32.5 kph. It was lovely to reacquaint myself with landmarks from the previous summer that I had assumed I would never see again: the supermarket in Honningsvåg where I had my final meal before firing up to the finish of the North Cape 4000; the farm outside Alta where Louise and I spent a few days surrounded by a hundred howling sled-dogs while I recuperated after that previous event.

My first day's riding had started at midday, and after just over 8 hours of riding I was back in Alta. I realised how quietly ridiculous it was for me to get off the bus at North Cape and immediately retrace the exact same route back to where I had boarded it that morning. Because this was such a short day, I scaled back my sleep to compensate and paused only for a brief nap rather than a proper overnight stop. I was back on the road the next morning at 0115. How incredibly convenient the Arctic summer sunlight was! Riding in the small hours of the morning was as easy as riding in the middle of the day.

The landscape up in Finnmark was as remote and as beautiful as I remembered it from the previous year. It is so desolate up there that the road would occasionally broaden

out to twice its usual width so that it could be used as an air-
strip in emergencies. That region is so void that even the
most inconsequential landmark was announced as though it
were a metropolis. There was a location that second day – I
can't remember its name, so let's say it was 'Flurgen' – that
did this memorably. After long quiet hours of seeing nothing but lakes and small stunted trees, I spotted a sign announcing 'Flurgen: 79 km'. *Ooh*, I thought, *a chance to see
something that's not a tree.* I began over the following hours to
count down the signs: Flurgen: 69 km, Flurgen: 59 km... By
the time I reached the sign announcing there were only 9
kilometres to go I was practically bouncing on the saddle
with excitement.

It was a fence. They had signposted a fence from 79 kilometres away.

There really is *nothing* up there in Finnmark.

The wildness of this landscape was fascinating to experience. The air of Finnmark is so crisp and clean that it makes
you regret every lungful you have ever breathed before. A
single car running ten metres away reeks like a burning
mattress. As you wrinkle your nose in shock and distaste,
you cannot help but reflect on how often you have inhaled
that filth in the past without even noticing. Once you have
tasted purity, everything else is compromise.

But the remoteness of Finnmark had made my planning
more difficult. Knowing just how few opportunities there
were to resupply up here – especially on the third day of
the ride, which fell on a Sunday – I had planned meticu-
lously which shops I would be able to visit for the first few
days, and had estimated arrival times for each. Many hours
had been spent working out this route on a spreadsheet. My
mantra throughout the previous months had been 'Think at
home, not on the road'. Knowing the time pressure I would
feel when riding, and how tired I was likely to become after
a few days, I had done my best to reduce the mental side of
the ride down to nothing more than following a trail on my

bike computer and stopping when I reached food shops that I had scouted out in advance.

Comforted by these preparations, the first couple of days saw me soar, unleashed after so many months of anticipation. The wind initially stayed largely at my back and I continued to fly down Norway and into Finland at a great pace. My good mood continued even as the Arctic started to make things tougher. The temperature dropped, and then persistent rain set in. Resigned to being wet and cold – what else had I expected up here? – I put my head down and cruised along the largely deserted roads, stopping every few hours in bus shelters or in the doorways of shuttered shops to assemble cheese sandwiches. To take a break from the solitude and stillness of these hours I started listening to a collection of PG Wodehouse stories, but I found the frothy inconsequence of Bertie Wooster's adventures were ill-fitting to this wild landscape and to my daunting endeavour. I switched it off after a few chapters and listened instead to the sound of the north wind.

oOo

Deprived of anything to look at other than trees and grass, I spent long hours staring at my own hands as they pointed out in front of me on the aerobars. After a while, I began to notice my hands were becoming visibly puffy and swollen. *Shit*, I thought, dimly remembering an article I had once read about the risks of endurance sport: *swollen hands are a sign of salt imbalance.* But I couldn't remember whether swollen hands indicated too much salt in the body or not enough. Why couldn't I remember this? Was forgetfulness another warning sign? Was I was riding oblivious into some catastrophic meltdown from having too little and/or too much salt in my body? I worried gently about this for a couple of hours before realising that I had been wearing arm warmers ever since setting off from North Cape. What

I was seeing was the result of having my wrists squeezed by tight fabric tubes for the past two days. This is the sort of thing that happens when the mind is allowed to run free.

The previous year, on the North Cape 4000, I had usually arrived into towns at the end of a day's riding long after midnight. I had pushed deep into the nights to get more distance under my belt and separate myself from my pursuers, riding for as long as I felt possible before snatching a short rest. But this ride would be different. A clock is circular, with a beginning and an end wherever we decide to place them. With no need to follow other people's schedules, I shifted my days around to arrive early and leave early. My second night on the road saw me roll into the Finnish town of Pello before 8 o'clock, after 432 kilometres riding. Arriving early in the evening meant the logistics became so much easier than if I had arrived at midnight or beyond, as I would have done in the past: the hotel reception was open, as was a nearby shop and a pizza restaurant. I was able to buy the next morning's food, eat a pizza, upload a progress video to Twitter and then get into bed, all in under an hour. At 0215 the next day I was back on the bike enjoying completely empty roads while everybody else slept. I had ridden over a hundred kilometres before the rest of Finland had even eaten breakfast. What a delight. So successful was this tactic of 'arrive early, leave early' that I stuck with it as much as possible throughout the rest of the ride. Although never quite as convenient as in the Arctic, where my early-morning starts were in full daylight, the approach was easily one of the best tactics I ever discovered for this kind of riding.

oOo

Pckssssh-vrrrrrh.

I bounced up and down impatiently on my toes, waiting for the vending machine to finish whirring and present me with my coffee. It was early on the third day of my ride and I had recently crossed out of the Arctic. Ironically, almost as soon as I had officially left the Arctic the weather had become more challenging. The wind had swung around so it was no longer behind me, then the temperatures had dropped and it had begun to rain again – a heavy, dense rain that fell for hours. Even layered up with thermals and a jacket, I was shivering until I found a petrol station that was open early and selling coffee. I dripped dry with my hands clutched around the cup to restore life to my fingers. Despite the conditions, I am pleased to say that I was disciplined enough to leave in no longer than the planned thirty minutes of my break.

Even without any tailwind, my fitness and enthusiasm meant I flew that day. Hunched low on the aerobars, I set a series of top-10 segment times on Strava as I put in the klicks across Finland to complete a 453-kilometre leg. So far did I travel from north to south that I passed right into a new climactic zone. The day began with me shivering in the Arctic and it ended with me smothered in sunscreen. It was disconcerting to see such rapid change when moving under my own power. Bicycles are incredible.

My path again hit last year's North Cape 4000 route. I first found myself touching old ground when I passed through the city of Oulu, where I was joined for a short time by a friendly local resident whom I know from Instagram. Then, in the afternoon, I had a weird incident of deja vu as I walked into a roadside supermarket in Siikalatva. I stood still for a few seconds, feeling confused and dislocated, until I realised that I genuinely *had* been in that shop before, but had failed to noticed that my route overlapped at this point with last year's. I recovered from the experience by childishly taking photographs of Finland's FANNY milkshakes in the refrigerators.

From that point, my spirits were dampened first by growing headwinds, and then by problems with my bike computer. Approaching the small town of Iisalmi at the end of the third day, my computer began to display some of the issues that would plague the rest of this ride. I relied on this computer both to show me my planned route and to record my progress as evidence for the Guinness Records people. Although my phone could also do both of these jobs if necessary, it would not be as convenient as using a dedicated cycle computer: the phone was not waterproof, and was not intended to have its screen running all the time.

I had owned this bike computer for a couple of years and had tested it on many adventures in the past, including the Transcontinental and the North Cape 4000. Apart from the time it had been struck dumb by the clocks going back in the middle of an overnight ride, it had generally performed just fine. But for reasons that I do not understand, it did not like this latest trip. Towards the end of that third day, as I approached Iisalmi, it crashed abruptly – not for the first time that day – and I had to stand at the side of the road for ten minutes or more watching it very slowly recover the data from that day's ride so far. I could not just keep moving and wait for it to reboot while I rode, as that would risk losing some of the valuable tracker data that I would need to submit to Guinness as proof of my ride. I didn't think they would take kindly to seeing big unexplained leaps in the recorded track. Instead I had to stand there by the roadside, watching the computer's agonisingly slow reboot progress: 'RECOVERY 17% COMPLETE...' (Glaciers sweep in and out of the valleys; civilisations rise and fall; the Sun expands into a red giant and swallows the Earth...) 'RECOVERY 18% COMPLETE...'

Then, as I got even closer to Iisalmi, the computer stopped displaying the map. Normally, it would show a map of the road network with my planned route overlaid as a series of arrows. But that day, the background road map abruptly disappeared, leaving me staring at a blank page with nothing but a few arrows on it. Stripped of context, my intended path was difficult to follow – especially in built-up areas where I often had to do U-turns after discovering I had chosen the wrong turning where several roads met. It was all quite troubling. *I always knew there would be setbacks*, I told myself. *I just didn't know what they would be.*

The day ended with a final series of frustrations in a quietly shambolic hotel in Iisalmi. The reception had closed earlier than advertised, meaning I had to phone a security guard to come and let me in. This guard, while friendly and keen to help, didn't know how to handle payments and asked me to pay when I departed in the morning. But I was going to be back on the road long before the next day's re-ceptionist arrived, and this led to a whole load more time wasted while the guard got in touch with the hotel manager and the manager travelled across town to process my bank card. As this farce unfolded, I had to resist the urge to hop from one foot to the other, deeply aware of precious time dribbling away. Every minute wasted was a potential minute added to my ride time, putting me a minute closer to not breaking the record. And a lot of minutes were wasted that night.

Russia

Day four, and my computer issues continued to trouble me. At first, everything looked promising when the maps ab-ruptly reappeared on the screen as I was leaving Iisalmi, but then they disappeared again a couple of hours later and stayed gone. Back at home, Louise had the idea of contact-ing the manufacturer's Public Relations team and telling them about the problems I was having while undertaking a world record attempt. I suspect she exaggerated my ability to say bad things about their product to a lot of dotwatch-ers, because somebody from the manufacturer called al-most at once. I spoke to him through my earphone while riding through the endless forest. While keen to help, the man who called had never encountered this problem before and was not able to solve it. The entire rest of my ride to Spain was done while looking at a string of arrows that pointed down invisible roads on a completely blank screen. I would end up doing a lot of U-turns across Europe. I had to remind myself not to be thrown by this. *I always knew there would be setbacks*, I told myself again, as though repeating a mantra.

For hours the route took me through a long green ribbon of uninhabited taiga: lakes, pines, firs and silver birch, drifting past over and over in every permutation. The dense network of lakes in this part of Finland had formed in a series of rolling depressions. It was like riding across a vast eggbox, and for over three hundred kilometres I went up and down a procession of surprisingly steep little hills to cross from one basin to the next. A substantial detour around a closed stretch of road slowed me down further, especially as I could not see the roads on my computer and, once away from my planned route, had to check maps on my phone at every junction. *I always knew there would be setbacks.*

As I rode through these long stretches of bristling pines, I prepared myself for the part of this journey I feared most: the border crossing into Russia. From accounts written by other cyclists, I knew that getting into Russia takes ages and the guards make your life hell for the time they have you in their hands. You must go through paperwork multiple times; are made to answer a series of repetitive, intrusive questions; and have to empty every last item out of your bags for inspection. It is a formalised display of power and control by a huge, centralized state. I had specifically allowed several hours for this crossing when planning my ride and so, although the delays would be annoying, they would not throw off my schedule unless I got a particularly difficult border guard who spun things out all day.

My greater fear, of course, was being refused entry into the country altogether. I had no backup plan for that, and so dealt with the concern by not thinking about it.

I rolled up to the border station, leaned my bike against a wall and walked inside. I handed my passport to a guard, who licked his thumb and began slowly to leaf through the pages. *Flrrp. Flrrrrp.* Eventually he reached the page with my Russian visa and glanced up at me.

'Saint Petersburg?' he asked.

'*Da*,' I nodded, exhausting literally half my Russian vocabulary. The other half was '*nyet*' – 'no'.

The guard handed my passport back and waved me into the country.

It was that easy to get into Russia.

I sent Louise a text message as I rolled around the loops of road behind the border station. 'I'm in!' I typed while pedalling. 'That was EASY.'

The road rounded a long curve and then, up ahead, I spotted another border post. This one was flying the Russian flag. I glanced back at the building I had just left and noticed, for the first time, that it was flying the Finnish flag.

'I might have spoken too soon,' I typed as I rolled through no-mans-land.

The real Russian control point was a small cluster of buildings scattered around some branching roads and a truck-park. Signs directed me to the central area of the compound where a handful of cars and vans were parked up outside one of the buildings, clearly going nowhere. One of the vans was positioned over an inspection pit sunk into the road. The vehicles' occupants stood around in twos or threes, leaning against walls, smoking, resigned to a long wait. This was a bad sign. I couldn't even work out which building I was supposed to approach.

Just then, a rattling metallic noise caught my attention. I looked around to see a young woman on a rusty yellow bicycle approaching from behind. Riding an old bike without any luggage, she was clearly a local. I instantly glommed onto her like a leech. She pulled up outside one of the buildings and leant her bike against the wall. I gestured to her questioningly – *Me too? Should I leave my bike here?* She nodded and disappeared into the building. I followed close behind.

The passport and visa check took less than five minutes. The young woman's passport, I noticed, was packed full of identical entry and exit stamps, dozens on each page. It looked like she was a Russian with a job in Finland. The guard stamped my passport then handed it back to me and turned his gaze away, no longer interested. I was unsure what happened next. Did I go to another part of the compound for the next part of the process? When did they root through my luggage? Would there be a strip-search? I glanced over at the young woman, who gestured impatiently towards a door that led out of the building and into Russia. I made a questioning face and then mimed collecting my bike and riding over the border. *Yes, yes*, she nodded, waving again at the door. Then she disappeared on her way.

It was, after all, as easy as that to get into Russia.

oOo

After the clean affluence of Finland, rolling into the Russian border town of Svetogorsk was a jarring experience. It was like a fever-dream of Europe, or something from dystopian science fiction: everything was recognisable, yet somehow not quite right. The streets had all the familiar components – roads, apartment buildings, cars – but everything was run down and chaotic compared to what it had been just a moment ago. Ageing vehicles bounced down broken streets, coughing dirty clouds of smoke into the air. Everything was familiar, yet alien. The flashing red and blue lights of the money changers' huts lent the scene a further air of disrepute.

Rob Gardiner, who had broken this same world record four days before I set off on my trip, had sportingly sent me a message to warn me what lay ahead. Just after the border,

he said, was fifty kilometres of bad roadworks. I left Svetogorsk worried about what I was going to find down the
road.

It was worse than I imagined.

The highway was being rebuilt in the most ridiculous way
possible. The sensible way to replace a road is to repair half
the carriageway at a time, so there is some useable surface
to be shared, in turns, between the northbound and southbound traffic. Here, however, they were replacing entire
long stretches of road all at once. A pair of traffic lights
would be erected perhaps 5 kilometres apart and placed on
a timer, switching over every 8 or 10 minutes to reverse the
traffic flow. The entire road between these points was then
dynamited down to the bedrock all at once. Vehicles getting
the green light would be left to pick their way through kilometres of craters and mud until they reached the waiting
queue of vehicles held by the traffic light at the far end.
There might then be a short stretch of not-quite-so-
shattered tarmac before the whole process began again,
with another five-kilometre section of destroyed road.

The system was probably fine if you were in one of the
many rusty old trucks that clattered around the place, and
was more or less passable in a car, as long as it belonged to
your worst enemy. But the arrangement provided a helpless
murder-zone for anyone on a bicycle.

Because progress over the shattered surface was so slow,
and because the traffic lights were placed so far apart, there
was no hope of getting to the other end of each controlled
zone before the lights changed. Instead, I would get a short
way into the zone, other vehicles clattering past me from
behind the whole time, before I would look up and find a
swarm of huge trucks bouncing towards me from up ahead.
I would scramble off the edge of the road and wait several
minutes – being devoured by mosquitoes the whole time –
until the distant traffic lights went red and I could begin to
move forward again. This would buy me perhaps one
minute of bouncing through the craters on my own before

another wave of motorised carnage caught up with me from behind as the previous traffic lights went green. Once more, I would be forced off the road to provide another mosquito buffet until eventually the traffic stopped and I had another minute before the steel tsunami started coming from in front again.

Only being able to move in the short windows between the forwards and backwards tides of traffic meant my progress was glacial. Much of the time, for this entire fifty-kilometre stretch, I was standing by the roadside, coughing on dust and having my blood syphoned out in tiny but unhelpful quantities by the insects that swarmed in from the surrounding forest.

I cannot express the relief I felt finally to get onto a proper road outside the small city of Vyborg. It was hours later than I had hoped to be here. As evening settled over the city, I rolled into the northern outskirts where I bounced around a series of low-rise tower blocks on ill-repaired side-streets until eventually I managed to find the entrance to the Kirovskije Dachi motel (I don't speak Russian, but I'm guessing Kirovskije Dachi translates as 'Badly Signposted'). It had been a long day of frustration and slow progress and I was aching to get into a bed. But first I had a more pressing problem: I had no food, there had been no shops on my way into the city, and I was deeply hungry, given all the time spent getting here from the border.

Thankfully, as I finished checking into the motel, I spotted a menu lying on the counter. I seized it like a drowning person grabbing at a life-ring in the ocean. The young receptionist darted forward with surprising reflexes and snatched the menu from my hand before I even had it fully open. '*Nyet!*' she admonished, exhausting the remainder of my Russian vocabulary.

'But I need food!' I bleated. I mimed eating and looked around helplessly, shrugging the question. The receptionist blinked slowly at me, unmoved, before gesturing to a stash of provisions that were on sale behind the counter. And thus it was that, a few minutes later, I tucked myself into bed with a bar of chocolate and a bottle of beer: a poor reward after a long, gruelling day in the saddle, and a woeful replacement for all the energy I had burned that afternoon.

oOo

The next morning, at quarter to four, I was back on the road amidst the ill-lit stillness of a crumbling city that was not yet awake. I was keen to get moving, but first I had to hunt for food. Cracked roads took me to Vyborg's McDonald's, which was supposed to be open early, but I found it locked up and dark when I arrived. A nearby 24-hour petrol station was also closed. This was ridiculous. I bounced down the carriageway, all alone in the sleeping city. I really didn't want to head out into the countryside without any breakfast, but equally I didn't want to lose hours hanging around in Vyborg waiting for businesses to remember their own opening times. Finally, at the far end of the city, I found a petrol station that was accepting customers. I drank coffee and ate a succession of sweet pastries as dawn broke over the concrete landscape outside.

Once outside the city, the roads began to improve and I had a pleasant few hours riding alone through still forests on quiet roads. There was a steady headwind, but it was gentle enough that it did not bother me particularly. After a while the forests thinned and I hit the coast near Zelenogorsk. With the placid waters tickling the shore to my right, I began to circle the edge of the huge bay that sits at the eastern edge of the Gulf of Finland. Through the haze, in the far distance on the other side of the sea, I could just make out a cluster of tall buildings. These marked my next major destination: Saint Petersburg. I was not looking forward to crossing such a vast city. I stopped at a petrol station and, with grim resignation, ate my first 7 Days croissants of the trip.

Saint Petersburg proved to be a game of two halves. The way into the city was surprisingly pleasant and easy. I picked up a roadside cyclepath near an outlying town called Lisy Nos, west of the city, and then cruised along at a fair pace, swapping between the cyclepath and the parallel road whenever the other looked better. I spotted a couple of local cyclists heading into the city on nice road bikes, and put on a little extra effort to try and match their pace. But with their fresh legs, I didn't stand a chance.

The cyclepath dropped me into the city amidst a huge new development near the Maritime Victory Park. Here were the towers I had spotted from across the bay that morning. It all felt prosperous, modern and impressive. From this outer edge of the city, I crossed the river into the older parts of the city and was impressed by what I found. I don't think I have seen another city with such a splendid riverfront. For the first time on this trip, I regretted my need for speed. Central Saint Petersburg looked magnificent and I immediately made a note to return one day.

At this point, I discovered Saint Petersburg was like a pitcher plant, or Venus fly trap, except specialised for catching cyclists rather than flies. You sense glorious promise in the centre and find the route in to be ever so easy... only to realise you are doomed after reaching the point of no return.

Months earlier, studying the map, I had seen that the obvious route out of the city was down a long straight road that headed southwest. It was the first big step on my way to the Estonian border, which I hoped to reach that afternoon. But getting to this road threw me into the centre of the trap. A city gets the traffic it builds for, and Saint Petersburg's vast highways are built for motorists to drive very fast in huge volumes. As I spiralled into the city centre, the intensity and the insanity of the traffic swelled. I went from peaceful streets at the northwestern side of the city into a swirling vortex of metal. All around me was honking, swerving traffic carnage. My head swivelled from side to side as though I was a paranoid meerkat, scanning for hazards as I lurched from one intersection to the next. Each time I made it through a set of traffic lights to the other side of the junction without dying, I took a moment to congratulate myself for this improbable achievement. It's hard to imagine how the roads of Saint Petersburg could have been more dangerous to a cyclist without the introduction of wild bears or landmines.

The problem was not so much the volume of traffic – although this was plentiful – as the reckless inattention of the drivers. I came through St Petersburg asking myself why Russian cars even had windscreens, given that nobody ever seemed to look out of them. It felt as though every driver I saw was gazing down at their phone, barely glancing at the road as they sped along. It was hardly a surprise when I heard a loud bang from my left and saw several cars smash into one another three metres from where I stood in the road waiting for the traffic lights to change. When the drivers climbed out of their cars, I noticed their exchange had the resigned appearance of a routine interaction. Details were exchanged with the same degree of passion seen whenever somebody posts a parcel.

After a while the road got so wide, fast and crowded that I passed the point where I found the threat acceptable. I clambered over the barrier and pushed my bike along the verge for a couple of kilometres to get to the other side of a huge cloverleaf intersection filled with speeding cages of death. I feared for the damage this gravelly walking was doing to the soft plastic cleats on my shoes, but in my frustrated and filthy mood, couldn't be bothered to dig out my cleat covers.

And then, almost imperceptibly, the vast sprawling outskirts of Saint Petersburg began to thin and I was on the A-180 highway heading west. The road with thick with dirty old trucks and their choking clouds of Diesel fumes but, free from the city, I never felt in any particular danger – these drivers seemed capable of piloting their vehicles in more or less straight lines. Indeed, after a while I found my-self getting so comfortable with the procession of trucks that I started veering towards each one as it pulled along-side so I could enjoy the brief low-pressure tug as it passed. This air-drag was enough to boost my speed by 2 or 3 kph for a few seconds. At that point, desperate to make progress after the slow passage through the city, I was happy to enjoy every one of these little tows and didn't really consider the risk of leaning into these 40-tonne monsters. It was only a lot later that I wondered at the wisdom of this.

Eventually I reached the control point at the Estonian border. There was a much greater mass of people crossing the border here than there had been at the Finnish side of the country, many on foot. The guards here were more har-assed and surly, I noted. I started to worry this border cross-ing was going to be a lot slower and more difficult than the last, but then I thought *What are they going to do – keep me here?* and at once found myself approaching the whole thing more bullishly. I was through Russia now; I no longer needed anything from this country. I strode into the painted cabin that housed the control and handed over my passport with a no-nonsense air. I was out the other side and into Estonia within a few minutes.

After all those months of trepidation, I had made it through Russia in not much more than a day.

Thanks a lot, Beaufort

The next day – Day 6, if I counted my shorter first section as a whole day – I crossed all of Estonia and most of Latvia. I did it at a good pace too. On the one hand, such strong progress after several days' riding showed I was successfully looking after my body and keeping myself in a position where I could keep putting out the big miles. But on the other hand, I was starting to store up problems that threatened to throw my record attempt into doubt.

Something else happened that day too: an important turning-point in my internal journey. I didn't realise it at the time, but this was the day when the initial phase of excitement passed and I started to experience the daunting reality of what I had bitten off by trying to break an ultradistance world record. It was the day when I had to start digging into my past experience of endurance racing to remember the strategies needed to deal with long-term suffering.

I started the morning at 0345 from a hotel in Johvi, a small town about two hours past the Russian border. I quietly carried my bike through some awkward fire doors and down a narrow flight of stairs to head out into the deserted pre-dawn gloom. I had reached the hotel too late for dinner the previous night and had been forced to beg the waitress for whatever she could possibly let me have to eat – three sickly-sweet cakes, it turned out. I had devoured these with little pleasure, a grim duty rather than a meal. I was craving something more substantial, and particularly a break from all the sugar I was living off. This had been the second evening in a row when I had finished riding too late to find proper food. Coming off the back of my choco-beer disappointment in Vyborg the previous evening, I was uncomfortably aware of how my planned daily routine was starting to slip.

Back in Finland, the tactic of 'start early-finish early' had been working well. But issues like my crashing computer, the roadworks in Russia and all the time lost crossing Saint Petersburg had started to eat into my days. I was no longer enjoying the convenience of finishing each stretch of riding in time to find food easily. This started to worry me, and I spent quite a lot of time thinking about how I might best get back onto schedule without losing valuable riding hours. Had I been too relaxed with my breezy plans for 400 kilometres a day? Should I have included some contingency?

Or had I been right to plan for the best case and just improvise around any problems as they arose? After all, my preparations had successfully got me through the most logistically difficult part of the ride in Norway and Finland. If I had given myself an hour of slack in the schedule each day, would I risk arriving in places too early if my days unfolded cleanly...? Thinking about all the permutations was frustrating. I would just have to wait and see whether my approach had been right or not. *For now*, I thought, *just ride the damned bike*.

oOo

My first morning in Estonia took me through a gently rolling landscape of firs, fields and wooden barns painted red in the Scandinavian style. Everything felt rustic and prosperous. The Estonian roads were as well-maintained as I remembered them from the previous year and the light asphalt spun slickly beneath my wheels. The audax hotels (bus shelters, to laypeople) were large, enclosed and clean, and I made a mental note in case I found myself needing somewhere to sleep.

After a while, my route turned southwest to take me around the edge of Lake Peipus – a small inland sea shared between Estonia and Russia. Distinctive octagonal fish stalls stood by the road at frequent intervals, shuttered and quiet at such an early hour. As the lake rolled past on my left and as the people of Estonia started to wake up and appear on the road, I found myself pushing into a gentle but insistent headwind. It was strong enough for me to be certain it was slowing my progress, but not quite strong enough to rustle the trees that lined the road: a '1' on the Beaufort scale of wind speed. Riding into such a stealthy breeze created a perceptual illusion: with nothing to betray the wind's presence to my eyes, I had a powerful sensation that I was pushing through air that was somehow a lot thicker than normal.

It was like stirring cream when you expected milk. I had ample time that morning to resent this: *if you're going to be windy, at least look windy*, I thought. Before long, this sly breeze quietly ushered in two days of intermittent rain that chilled me and drove me to seek warming cups of hot chocolate during my rest-stops. Three punctures, all in the rear wheel, made my schedule slip even further.

But it was not all problems that day. Perhaps the highlight was crossing the border from Estonia to Latvia early in the afternoon and immediately reacquainting myself with Latvia's one-kilogram bags of yoghurt. These are intended to last a family for a week, and so I received looks of naked disgust as I stood outside the supermarket in Valka, ripped the corner off the packet and slammed the entire contents in one lusty gulp. I wiped the back of my hand across my mouth then returned the villagers' stares with a smile – decorum be damned: I had managed to syphon over a thousand calories down my throat in under ten seconds and that was all that mattered. Then, to satisfy my craving for savoury food, I ate a tub of hummus and a whole loaf of wonderfully crusty bread. It was one of the most effective and pleasurable meals of the trip.

Focus

Latvia, I hoped, would be fast. When planning my route, I had deliberately made the decision to favour bigger, quicker roads over smaller, quieter roads almost every time there was a choice between the two. I was going for a world record and so speed had to be a key concern, even sometimes at the expense of safety – or, at least, comfort. Almost the whole of my route through this country was on big main roads including, notably, a stretch of motorway that was permitted to bicycles. It was all a world away from the dirt track I had taken through Latvia the year before. The straight flat roads eased my journey; I hardly had to pause for hours at a time. I became so focused on the steady business of moving forwards that day that I rode through the city of Valmiera without stopping, or even glancing around. Looking back, I couldn't tell you the first thing about the place. It was only my GPS records that told me I ever went there at all. It would not be the last city that I entirely failed to notice thanks to my all-enveloping concentration on making progress.

This intense and constant focus was, in many way, the price I had to pay for using faster roads. I normally ride long distances in a pleasant state of mental relaxation, the comfortable familiarity of sitting on a bicycle allowing me to do most of the work on autopilot with my conscious mind free to do its own thing. But here, the ceaseless roar of passing trucks meant I had to be hyper-vigilant. Losing focus, and drifting even half a metre to my left, might put me in danger. Drifting to the right was almost as bad, as I might slip off the edge of the road surface and crash like I had in Romania two years earlier. Not too far left, not too far right, yet no safe haven in the middle: even when tracking straight, I could not afford to hit a pothole or piece of debris. All this meant that I spent the entire day maintaining firm control over the bike and scanning the road ahead as if my life depended on it – which, in a very real sense, it did. Sustaining this level of intense mental focus for hours at a time was exhausting. There is a reason that people who have to maintain their attention professionally, like radar operators, work in very short shifts and take a lot of breaks.

The relentless need to concentrate, and the flatness of the roads, started to take a toll on my mood. I sat on the ground outside a small petrol station that afternoon, eating an ice cream and recording one of the short videos that I was posting on Twitter each day. So far, these videos had been chirpy and upbeat – light-hearted observations about what I had seen or done. Even my report of having no food in Vyborg had been presented as a funny anecdote. But my video

ENDLESS PERFECT CIRCLES   159

from Latvia that day had a more reflective, confessional tone:

> "I found my mood going up and down a bit today. It's inevitable on a ride this sort of length that you're going to have good spells and bad spells, and quite a bit of this afternoon through Latvia has been a bit of a drag. It's been a long, busy road that just goes on forever. It's a very tedious road, and you find your mood going up and down. And you find the ability to pedal well just goes up and down. Sometimes you're cruising along just fine, putting the power down, and then ten minutes later you feel all clunky and out of rhythm and slow, so I've alternated between fast spells and slow spells all day.
>
> "But that's going to happen! That's what happens on these long journeys. You have the rough with the smooth. I came into this knowing that you have bad days, and if this is as bad as it gets, frankly that's not too bad."

I didn't know it at the time, but this shift to a more intro-spective tone sparked a new interest from the dotwatchers following my journey. The way I started to share the diffi-culties I was facing – and, particularly, how I found ways to cope with them – was what everybody would later want to talk about.

Indeed, after getting several messages in response to my first video, I even put out a short update that evening. Look-ing weary, and with a revolting glob of mucus fighting its way out of my right nostril, I looked into the camera's tiny lens and explained:

> "It occurred to me that there are probably quite a lot of people watching these videos who aren't ul-tradistance athletes. So for you 'norms' out there,

I thought I'd better say a little bit about mental strategy for something like this.

"Today's been up and down – good spells, bad spells – and one of the things that becomes really essential when you're doing these sorts of events, especially this kind of distance, is you absolutely have to let bad things go. If you have a bad spell, and you're struggling for a while, then once that moment is over you've just got to forget it. You can't sit there thinking 'What's this done to my average time? What's this done to my average distance?' What's gone is gone, and it becomes so important not to dwell on the negatives because... they're *going* to happen, they *will* happen. And when they happen there's nothing you can do about it whatsoever."

I was now starting to draw on all the lessons I had built up over the previous few years of endurance sport. The very deliberate and conscious strategy of acceptance – *Hello, Pain, I was wondering when you'd show up* – was keeping me moving despite the growing difficulties.

As well as accepting my lot, I was also using my experience to keep myself in the moment, to avoid being swamped by thoughts of what lay ahead:

"The other thing you really can't dwell on is the future. A few times earlier today, especially when I was rolling along some quite grippy roads early on, I found myself wanting to think about Spain... And I absolutely had to clamp down on that. The moment I started to think about Spain, that was overwhelming. I've got to stay in the moment, just focus on the next little attainable target and not look at the big picture, because it's just *too* big."

Looking back, I am proud of how successfully I learned the hard lessons from my earlier successes and failures and then applied them to this, the hardest challenge of my life.

oOo

The plan was to get a short break from major roads in the outskirts of Riga, where my route left the A2 highway and took smaller roads through the edge of city until eventually I would pick up the A7 highway on the other side of the Daugava river a couple of hours later. But as I saw the tall buildings of Riga appear in the distance and start to inch towards me, I found I had little appetite for tackling a capital city in the early evening, especially so soon after the horrors of Saint Petersburg. Given the thought of all the stop-start traffic lights that would slow me down, and the young idiots that were sure to be speeding around in their cars as evening fell, I decided I would take my chances with the trucks. I made the snap decision to turn onto the A4 highway and bypass Riga altogether.

This decision meant I got no break from keeping myself hyper-alert. This added to the raw physical burden of riding hundreds of kilometres, and I could feel just how much I was fighting fatigue that day. I stopped for food and a caffeine hit at a petrol station near Amatnieki, and it took a lot of willpower to leave there and get back onto the road, especially after a chat with Louise left me feeling homesick. The pressure of the heavy traffic remained as I slipped from one roaring highway to another: the A4 to the A6 to the A5. Night was falling upon the land by this point, and my dynamo-powered red light stabbed out behind me into the growing gloom. I reached back and activated my backup flashing light in the hope of being even more visible to the drivers high up in the cabins of their swooshing trucks.

The pressure constantly to scan the road for hazards was twice as demanding now it was dark, and I was feeling wired from the effort. It was a relief when I finally sighted the motel that I had identified as my target for the day. The receptionist rolled her eyes and gave a loud sigh of annoyance when I asked to check in, as though my arrival meant she had just lost a bet. And once past her, I found my room was shabby and worn. But I didn't care about any of this. There was a shower and a bed, and that is all I needed. By that point, I would have been relaxed if I had found the bed missing. The motel room meant I could stop for a while, and that was the main thing.

I had started that morning at 0345 and now, 414 kilometres later, I ended my ride at 2300. So much for 'start early, finish early'. Headwinds, and the day's punctures, meant that my timing had slipped for the third day in a row. I was tempted to try to get back on schedule by cutting my sleep short that night, but then I remembered my lessons from the Transcontinental Race and decided this would be a false economy. I reminded myself that even though I looked and felt as if I had been on the road for weeks, I had in reality barely begun this journey. I couldn't afford to start cutting into my overnight recovery at this stage when I had so much riding still to go. With a sense of resignation I set my alarm for 0500 the next day, leaving me ready to hit the road at 0530 in line with my regular 6.5-hour overnight break schedule. The sun would be up at that time; this was nothing like the 2 o'clock starts I had managed back in Finland. I would just have to find some other way to sort out my schedule.

I took some small consolation from how the grumpy motel receptionist had let me bring my bike into my room, which was both convenient and reassuring. Indeed, with one exception that I will describe later, every hotel I visited during this trip allowed me to take my bike into my room. I firmly believe this is because of a Jedi mind trick I discovered on earlier rides: *never wheel your bike into a hotel, always carry it*. Wheeling your bike across the foyer makes receptionists recognize it as a vehicle, and start to issue unhelpful demands about storing it outdoors. But *carrying* the bike into a hotel seems to stop people realising what it is. When carried silently in your hands, the bike is just another piece of luggage and no questions are asked when you take it upstairs.

Carry, don't roll. It works every time.

Acceptance

It was a good job I was remembering my experiences of how to cope with long-distance racing because, although I didn't know it at the time, I was now heading into a far tougher period of this ride, one that would last for many days. The winds were building in the west, and would soon begin fiercely to oppose my progress. Getting through the next few countries would draw on all the coping I could muster.

That morning, however, I did not know about the difficulties ahead of me. I awoke in my Latvian motel and spent a few seconds savouring the stillness and peace before the incessant need to *push, push, push* kicked in for the day. Lying on my back in the darkness, I lifted my knees to my chest and wrapped my arms around my shins, pulling my legs into my chest and enjoying the sensation of stretching my back and glutes. Then I reached over to grab my phone from the bedside table so I could disable the alarm before it began to sound. I was so focused throughout this ride that, no matter how tired I was, I always woke exactly two minutes before my alarm went off. Right on schedule, thirty minutes after waking, I was rolling out of the sleeping motel's driveway and back onto the long straight road outside.

The morning that greeted me was wet and cold: crowded knots of grey beech trees dripped silently between the fields; the passing trucks swished through standing water on the carriageway. They carved brief dry trails that vanished within seconds as if the vehicles had never been there. Beginning to push towards the border with Lithuania, I dropped low onto the handlebars and set my face for action. The poor weather was disappointing, but the road surface was good and I felt surprisingly eager to ride again after just a few hours off the bike. The first hundred kilometres passed easily, almost without my noticing. *Sleep is amazing*, I thought, not for the first time.

A steady rain drummed on my helmet as the efficient highways led me southwest. These were long straight roads that pressed through endless fields of maize and mournful, brooding sunflowers. I rarely needed to change gear on these flat highways and my legs just mechanically pumped out the exact same motion at the exact same rhythm, ten thousand times every hour.

I stuck at this until reaching Krekenava, deep in Lithuania, where I crossed onto a smaller road that ran parallel to the main road on the other side of the Nevėžis River. I remembered this junction from my route planning sessions: the smaller road was the same length as the highway, and Google Streetview suggested it had a good surface, so I had diverted onto it. I thought that a couple of hours away from main roads would be a relaxing break. While sitting at my kitchen table and planning my route months earlier, I had thought of this route choice as a gift to my future self.

It was everything I hoped for. The road was free of traffic, and its surface was almost as smooth and fast as the highway I had abandoned. I never normally listen to music when I cycle – I listen to audiobooks or podcasts when I want something in my ears – but that day I had the urge for some tunes and so started a playlist of upbeat songs as I joined the smaller road. The music was perfect for my buoyant mood. I sang out loud, my voice travelling unashamedly across the fields of waving cereals. I was delighted by the experience of having the road entirely to myself. I hadn't realised how much I had been oppressed by all the motor traffic until it was gone.

Barely perceptible slopes rolled up and down along the edge of the river's floodplain. These took me through one amber wheatfield after another, broken from time to time by thin strands of low trees, their branches beginning to wave in a stiffening breeze. An occasional single-story farmhouse appeared by the road, hushed and still. The rain had stopped and, although the sun was not quite out, there was a promise of brightness in the air. I sang and danced in the saddle as small sleepy hamlets whipped by. This road was so quiet that the occupants' dogs roamed free. Passersby were rare, and so these dogs were not primed to attack. The occasional animal that decided to go for me was far too slow to react, and I dropped them easily behind my whirling wheels. After two previous trips across eastern Europe I was an old hand at outrunning dogs; these hairy boys didn't stand a chance.

The wheatfields rippled and pulsed in the breeze as I swooped down the fast, quiet roads, happily immersed in my music. And then I hit a long stretch of roadworks and the whole morning fell apart. I found that the Lithuanians use the same stupid system of smashing up their roads as the Russians. The section under repair here seemed endless, and the rough, potholed surfaces gave me two punctures, one right after the other. It started to rain again as I stood by the muddy roadside changing my tubes. The long delays at the temporary traffic lights made the motorists impatient to make back the lost time when we were finally released to move again. Generally we were all able to co-exist as we picked our ways over the broken roads, but a couple of the more aggressive drivers expected me somehow to evaporate and leave the shattered roads to them alone; one practically nudged me off the road with his crappy old car, the entitled prick.

This stretch of stop-start traffic and slow riding must have cost me at least two hours. Always aware of the ever-ticking clock, and my slipping schedule, it would have been easy to get frustrated or angry at this. But I found I could still summon the calm acceptance that had come into play the previous day. The next of my short video updates picked up on this:

> "I've just had a really nasty stretch of roadworks that went on for ages and I lost quite a lot of time. And I had a puncture. But what can you do? There was no way to know it was there. I'd have stayed on the main road if I had known there were going to be roadworks but… hey, if it's done it's done."

No recriminations, no frustration, no shaking my fist at my past self and his stupid route. Would I have remained so calm if I had not calculated my average progress so far at 407 kilometres per day? Would I have handled the loss of time quite so well if I had not been clearly moving faster than the current world-record pace? I'm not sure. I like to think that I would have said 'It's only riding a bike, after all'. But I cannot say for certain this would have happened, at least not right then, and perhaps not for a long while after. I had invested too much in this venture to shrug off failure so readily. But thankfully all this was moot that day: my training and fitness meant that my progress over the first six days had been strong. For now at least, I could afford to stay in the present and accept mishaps that were outside my control with the placid resignation they needed.

The bigger challenge that day was the wind. It built throughout the afternoon until by four o'clock it looked as though a giant invisible hand was swiping at the grass and grappling with the trees. I was running 50-mm deep wheels on my bike to get an aerodynamic advantage. These were excellent, but could become twitchy and unstable when strong winds caught them from the side. Accordingly, my day took a turn for the worse when I joined the highway from Marijampolė to the Polish border. This road was the most obvious option for crossing into Poland – both for me and, more regrettably, about five million trucks every hour. Rob Gardiner, a couple of weeks earlier, had found this road excessively stressful and had warned me to avoid it if possible. But his warning came too late: to redirect this leg of the journey would have involved rethinking my entire route across Latvia, Lithuania and Poland. I simply did not have time to do that in the final days before my departure.

Anyway, how bad can it be? I thought as I joined the highway and headed south. I had spent plenty of time over the past few days on major roads, ever since the stretch between Russia and Estonia. These had not been relaxing, and at times had required all my concentration, but I had found enough space in the shoulders at the edge of each road to keep myself far enough from the passing traffic. The highlight had been the Latvian motorway, where I had a full lane to myself, but even on roads where the white line at the edge marked off only half a metre of shoulder, I found this was just enough to maintain a bit of separation between me and the motorists. But this road from Marijampolė in Lithuania to Suwałki in Poland was ridiculously narrow for the volume of traffic it carried, and consequently there was no space at the edge at all. The thundering trucks were practically nose-to-tail the entire way and here I was, weaving in and out of the tiny gaps between one forty-tonner and the next, all the time slowed down by a blustery headwind that was growing in ferocity.

If Latvia's highways had required me to dig into my stores of mental focus the day before, that road to Poland required a whole lot more. I was exhausted from the stress of being immersed in such dense traffic when, eventually, I reached Suwałki and got onto some smaller roads. All the effort meant I was still twitchy and wired three hours later as I rode up and down the road into Grajewo, growing increasingly alarmed by how difficult it was to find the hotel I had booked that afternoon. I had ridden 408 kilometres and it was now around 2230. This was not quite the triumph it sounds. I had ridden my target daily distance and was finishing my ride with the clock showing a slightly earlier time than it had the night before – but I had crossed a time zone in the process. This meant that last night's sleep and this day's ride had together taken slightly over 24 hours. My rate of progress was objectively not bad, given all the roadworks, punctures and fear that I had dealt with along the way, but it was still more than 24 hours between the end of one day's riding and the end of the next, and so my schedule had slipped further. The day had also taken another big toll on my mind and I was aware of tapping into reserves that could not last indefinitely. I needed to recharge again so I could start to try and pull some time back tomorrow.

But first I had to locate this bloody hotel. How could it be so hard to find?! I turned on my phone and pulled up Google Maps for perhaps the fifth time in the last ten minutes. I zoomed in on the map as far as possible. The hotel was *right here*, it said, right where the glowing blue dot marked my position. But as I scanned around in the darkness it was clear that the hotel symbol on the map was in the wrong place. All I could find was some sort of tractor dealership, shuttered up and eerie in the darkness. I spent another fifteen minutes searching fruitlessly up and down the edge of town before I gave up. I reluctantly abandoned the money I had already committed for my hotel room and began to look for a bus shelter or some other hollow in which to bivvy. I spotted a dark gravel track heading away from the road. *Perhaps there'll be somewhere I can sleep up here*, I thought. And there was: the gravel track led right to my hotel. What a stroke of luck.

Poland

> "I'm just about to head out on the road for the morning. I think today's the day where I'm first really feeling the *size* of this. I did the maths last night and realised that even at the end of today, I'm not quite half-way. And given that I'm feeling really quite tired at the moment, that brought home to me just how enormous this challenge is."

It was 0550. I sat on my Grajewo hotel bed, my jersey half-fastened, doing a short update video. My face was visibly puffy and tired.

> "It didn't help morale yesterday when there was really really bad wind. It wasn't quite in my face *all* the time, maybe a bit came from the side, but it certainly spent quite a lot of time in my face and made for quite a tricky end to the day – I was crawling along at 20 kilometres an hour on what should be a main road. But... what can you do? Today's another day. It looks sunny, which is going to be pleasant... All I can do it get out there and keep moving. As long as I keep moving, I get to the end."

My morning routine was already established. Waking up and throwing myself into a rehearsed series of actions was already almost as automatic and inevitable as breathing or blinking. My eyes were barely open before I was strapping on my heart rate monitor and pulling on my shorts and jersey. Usually this was all done while mechanically eating whatever I had managed to buy for breakfast the day before, but the easy availability of food in Poland meant I had skipped my shopping the previous evening, deciding I would treat myself by hitting a petrol station as the first task of the day.

I left the sleeping hotel in Grajewo and remounted the bike. *How malleable time is*, I thought as I began to ride through the slowly awakening town. The journey so far had taken around a week, yet it felt like a year. Devoting myself entirely to this ride, and thinking about nothing else for 24 hours a day, had ballooned the task within my perception. I could barely remember *not* riding across Europe by this point. In many ways this is exactly what I had wanted back when I first read about the Transcontinental Race – I had wanted to discover what it was like to put my normal life on hold and give myself over entirely to some vast undertaking. Now here I was, deep in the reality of this wish. The ceaseless need to move fast now I was making a record attempt made it even more all-enveloping than I had ever experienced before. The cool air of the morning slipped easily over my shoulders as I relaxed onto the handlebars and began to put down the power.

oOo

Later, I would decide that I enjoyed Poland a lot more during this record attempt than I had on the North Cape 4000 ride the previous year. Back then, the organisers had routed us on some pretty grim little roads that had been broken and patched up badly. It felt at the time as though Polish roadworks were only ever done late on Friday afternoons, the tarmac slopped into each pothole with a shovel and left to stand proud of the road. Several stretches of that route had even been cobbled, which was particularly testing after many days of sitting on the saddle. The difficult progress soured my experience of the place, and I had found myself becoming critical. I had become particularly fixated on Poland's lack of public amenities like litter bins and benches, and had left the country feeling relieved to have got out into Lithuania.

This year was far better. I was on good roads, which helped. I also found Poland to be a fundamentally *convenient* place to cycle. Over the next couple of days I noted how practically every village had a food shop, and hotels and motels were plentiful and cheap. This all meant that the logistics of cycling across Poland were easier than in any other country on this trip. I could ride without concern, confident that food and lodging would never be difficult to find.

But these discoveries about Poland's positive qualities came later. On that first morning, the country was a trial. This was entirely down to the persistent wind, which had grown even stronger overnight and was now roaring squarely into my face. I dropped as low as I could on the aerobars, but the impact on my speed was still obvious. I know my own riding: I know how fast I should be going for any given effort level, and my speed here was far lower than what it should be. The wind was an invisible arm, forever shoving me backwards as if the West were forbidden to me. Polish national flags snapped and thrummed in each town as I passed, their thinnest ends pointed straight at me, taunting; their flaccid vibrations were like tongues blowing raspberries.

Riding into wind is not like climbing a hill; wind takes but never gives back. That morning, already feeling tired when I hit the road, I was finding it a challenge to make any progress and my morale started to sag. My glacial passage through the fields of bowing sunflowers meant I had many hours to contemplate what I was doing and ask myself why why why. *Why put yourself through this? Why does this matter so much to you? Why not just stop?* I was digging deeper into my reserves of coping. At times, the wind was so ferocious that I had to break the task down to its most basic level, focusing on nothing but the next roadside marker-post. Each of these posts was achieved only after its own drawn-out battle against the elements. I was crawling pathetically across the full width of Poland, fifty metres at a time. My knees started to ache from the grind; this was like a climb that never stopped. I was at a low point of the ride.

And then I was fine. Somehow, suddenly, along an anonymous road amidst the rolling plains of central Poland, everything was fixed in an instant.

I have experienced the turnabouts of ultradistance sport many times – the inexplicable swings from low to high or from high to low – but never as suddenly or as profoundly as that day in Poland. My reward for enduring through the winds all morning was for me to be infused, as if from nowhere, with a new strength. At once my legs were filled with fire. The numbers on my power meter started to creep up, as did my speed. I went from grovelling along the road to... well, if not flying up it, then at least riding along it much more happily and confidently. My body relaxed, my legs falling into a smooth rhythm, perfectly aligned with the needs of my machine. The power from my body was pumping efficiently into the wheels, driving me forward into the face of the elements.

I will always be humbled by the body's ability to find new reserves, to never quite reach rock-bottom. How can it be possible to go from feeling entirely beaten to feeling, moments later, right back on form? Clearly it is best not to question this mystery too far. Surely it is better to focus on what we can control: just keep moving, just keep eating, and stay strong. If the mind endures, the body will sooner or later catch up.

That afternoon I sat on a windowsill outside a petrol station and made another short video, trying to put my thoughts into some sort of order after experiencing this sudden and profound turnaround:

> "I just wanted to do a quick follow-up to this morning. Because I woke up feeling pretty awful today and, as several of you pointed out, I looked it as well.
>
> "Thanks for that.

"There was a strong temptation not to get back on the bike this morning, to just roll over and go back to sleep. I felt pretty awful after pushing through the winds last night. The reason I was able to get back on the bike, even though all this morning was slow and painful and I made very little progress, was I knew from doing this sort of thing before that, as long as I just kept doing something simple, it would work out. I can't think about being in Spain, but I can think about getting to the end of the road, I can think about small achievable goals: just turn the pedals; just keep turning them and sooner or later things will work out.

"Just now, as I've been cruising along at an incredible pace – more powerfully than I have for the last four days, which is *evidence* that if you just keep going, things work out – I've been thinking about something that the runner Ann Trason said. She said that running a hundred miles is like living your life in a day. And it occurred to me that – if this doesn't sound too over the top! – you only get one go at life, but doing things like this is the nearest you'll get to having a practice. You can test out strategies for coping with difficulty in a fairly safe environment. You can test them for real and see with your own eyes that strategies like focusing on sub-goals, staying focused on processes, and keeping going and waiting for things to turn around... you can see that these strategies do work. And that's one of the reasons I love ultraendurance sport."

Poland rewarded me for my tenacity with gifts both temporal and spiritual. A delivery driver smiled and handed me a chocolate bar as a I sat eating on the steps outside a small supermarket. Then, after I crossed the broad waters of the

Vistula river near Płock, the afternoon began to mellow into a glorious golden evening. Scattered wind-turbines whipped the air as I pushed westward through fields of ripe wheat, my new-found strength standing up proudly to the haughty wind. I was overcome with a profound delight in what I was doing. Enjoying a moment of awe, I again muttered *To think I might never have done this!* I took an over-excited number of photographs, and atmospheric videos of the road running free beneath my wheels as the sun set to my side.

Eventually I pulled into Bar Europa on Highway 92 near Koło and carried my bike up the stairs to a functional little motel room. It was 23 hours since I had stopped the previous night and I had ridden 353 kilometres. I was riding unsupported, and had to adapt to wherever the accommodation happened to be; sometimes this meant my days were longer or shorter than a strict 24 hours. For this reason, I made adjustments to measure my progress more fairly. That evening, my accounting went like this: it had been 23 hours since I ended the previous day's riding and my moving pace since then had averaged 26.3 kilometres per hour. To make my actual 23 hours comparable with a full day, I needed to add one more imaginary hour's riding. In this case, adding an extra 26.3 kilometres to my total meant I had been riding at roughly 380 kilometres in 24 hours. This was below the 400 kilometres I wanted to complete each day and, perhaps, I should have been more annoyed at myself for dropping below it... but I didn't really feel it at the time. The winds had been awful, and the morning had been hard. In the face of these trials, a distance of 380 kilometres in 24 hours didn't seem too bad. I dropped off to sleep on slightly damp sheets feeling content just to lie still for a short time. I even managed to sleep through the unwatched children shouting in the corridor outside my room.

It was only much later, reviewing the ride data as I wrote this, that I started to feel more ambivalent about that day's performance: 26.3 kph had been a good pace into a headwind with a week's fatigue in my legs but, at the same time, I had only averaged 26.3 kph when I was actually moving, which was far from the entire day. Just 13 hours and 26 minutes had been spent riding, out of 16 hours and 12 minutes since I had set off. The ideal day saw me stopped for 90 minutes: the total of my three thirty-minute breaks. In reality it was never quite as low as 90, because there would be various little extra patches of time added on from stopping at traffic lights, or briefly pulling over at the side of the road to attend to some small task or other. So a few extra minutes here or there were to be expected. But that day in eastern Poland I was stationary for over 160 minutes. On top of my three planned breaks, there had been an additional long stop for breakfast because I hadn't bought food the night before, plus two ten- or fifteen-minute petrol station raids for extra snacks to boost morale. These breaks were understandable, given the difficulties of the day, but they were also not in the plan. I had to do better than this. And if I ever create a time machine, I'll go back and tell myself, because I didn't really notice at the time.

Half-way there

If I thought I was going to avoid any more delays the next day, I was mistaken.

I said goodbye to the night porter and stepped out of the motel into the chilled darkness outside. Poland was silent as I started to ride through the dense woodlands that lined the road, my headlamp creating a bright path down the empty carriageway ahead of me. Once again, breakfast was eaten in a petrol station a short way along the route. Looking back as I write this, I wonder why I was not buying breakfast the night before to save time, as I had done in the first few days. I suspect I was unconsciously rewarding myself for my perseverance by giving myself a familiar cup of hot coffee to start of the day. I wanted these little treats badly at the time, but it was self-indulgent when I was supposed to be pushing for a record. The coffee should have waited until I got to my first planned break, the reward all the greater for having been postponed.

But the bigger time-sponge that day was the bike. As the half-way point of my journey would be somewhere in Poland, I had always intended to replace my chain here before it stretched too much. I found a bike shop In Jarocin, where I bought a new chain and a few spare inner tubes. Borrowing the shop's workstand, I had the chain installed on my bike within five minutes. I spun the pedals to see whether the gears needed a quick bit of fine-tuning after the change. *Hmm*, I thought. The chain was making a subtle noise as the pedals turned, a deep *thrum* that hadn't been there before. It wasn't a catastrophic sound, as though something were snarled up or broken, but... it wasn't quite right either.

I waved to the man behind the counter and he came over. I turned the pedals and he immediately picked up on the noise. Something was definitely not right. The man fiddled for a while, perplexed. After a couple of minutes he summoned his colleague, who also listened and fiddled, able to detect that something was amiss, but not able to pin down the cause.

And between the three of us, we never worked out what it was. My suspicion was always that the pins on this new chain stood slightly too proud, and so were rubbing against the sprockets on either side on the the one it was riding upon. But who knows? The men in the shop certainly didn't. 'Perhaps it will stop after a few kilometres?' said the first man. We all avoided one another's gaze so as not to acknowledge this vile and flagrant lie.

Deciding I preferred a small inexplicable noise to a large explicable delay, I left the shop and got back onto the road. With the wind in my ears I could not hear the chain's complaints, but I was aware of a gentle grinding sensation through the pedals that had not been there before, especially when I pressed hard. As if I didn't have enough to worry about already.

That wasn't the only issue with the bike that day. I also had a whole series of punctures – the first of them puncturing again about 500 metres after I had replaced the tube. Fixing all the flats that day cost me at least an hour. Polish roads had a striking amount of broken glass all over them, and I suspected this was to blame for the bursts. The nation's petrol stations sell a great many bottles of beer and vodka, and presumably a lot of these end up being thrown out of car windows. The process by which Polish drivers find themselves holding empty beer or vodka bottles while they are driving on the same roads as me was something I didn't want to think about too closely until I was safely out of the country.

The headwind was strong again today, perhaps even the strongest it had been so far. It had been such a relentless feature of my life these past few days that Stockholm Syndrome was kicking in and I was starting to accept – indeed, expect – the constant abuse of my tormentor. A few more days of this and I might start to see an angry, blustery headwind as a simple fact of life, no more to be resented than gravity is resented when climbing a hill. But just in case I was getting too comfortable with my lot, a new challenge appeared that morning. The sun, bored of ripening the endless fields of wheat and maize, turned its gaze my way. Sweat pooled in the brow of my helmet and salt began to form white crystals on the fabric of my jersey. Finding water became a much more urgent concern than it had been so far.

Set against these various trials, there was one huge triumph that day: I passed the half-way point of the journey. I really needed this emotionally, and had been counting down the kilometres. The jump from riding distances of around 4000 kilometres in previous years to riding over 6000 kilometres involved a leap beyond what was familiar. The previous two summers, I had passed the 3000-kilometre point knowing I was now approaching the finish and could afford to begin a collapse towards the line, leaving everything I had out on the course. But here, I passed that same 3000-kilometre milestone while not yet even half-way to the finish. There was no comforting collapse to reward me for getting here; I had to keep myself on top form so I could carry on cranking out the same performance day after day. After what felt like such a long time on the bike, I wanted reassurance I was truly making progress and would not just be spinning my pedals for eternity. The need to get into the second half of this ride was becoming urgent, its voice in my head like an impatient child: *are we half-way there yet? Are we half-way there yet?*

Eventually, finally, I watched the distance on my odometer reach the number that I had calculated as the divide between the eastern and western parts of my journey and I sagged with relief. There was a large signpost nearby, marking the beginning of a new county, and I used this as a handy backdrop for a short Twitter video cheerfully announcing that I had reached this watershed. 'It's all downhill from here!' I said, as I wrapped up the recording.

This was another monstrous untruth. In reality, the whole route to this point had been essentially flat. All of the big climbs were still ahead of me.

Always in the moment

Bent forever into the wind, I continued to push across the rest of Poland. The cracked grey tarmac of the roads flowed beneath my wheels, far slower than I would have liked, but at least it was moving. All I could do was just keep it in motion and hope that whatever speed I managed was fast enough. My way was lined with tall thin trees whose restless branches seemed always to be waving me backwards. *Why fight the wind?* they said. *It'll be so much easier if you turn around.* But not all the plants of Poland were so negative that day, and I was grateful to the massed fields of sunflowers who respectfully bobbed their heavy heads as I passed, quietly approving my efforts against the elements.

It was the ninth day on the road, but by now I could not have even have guessed what day it was. Time had no meaning any more. Always focused in the present, all that mattered was reaching the end of my current four-hour block of riding when I could pause for a short time to rest. These breaks were not glamorous – that day they were all picnics on petrol station forecourts amidst the puzzled stares of local motorists – but they each recharged my batteries just enough to get me through the next block. Less welcome were the involuntary breaks: a colander of punctures, and another big computer crash. The further I was into the day's riding when these crashes happened, the longer it took for the computer to recover all the data it had collected so far. That day's was after 300 kilometres of riding, giving me a frustrating 15-minute wait on the German border. I made use of the time by recording a short update video for Twitter.

> "What a day. Flippin' heck! Hours and hours of gruelling headwind has my speed down to *pathetic* levels. It was just shocking how slow I was going. And then a whole series of punctures... I think four or five in total and I spent so long faffing around with those. So yeah, it's been a slow day. I've just passed the 300-kilometre mark but... I'm actually feeling okay. I've been in good spirits all day and the body's feeling not too bad. I've got some food, so I'm going to press on for a while. Maybe there'll be a hotel somewhere convenient, otherwise I'll just sleep in the woods and nature can be my pillow for the night."

Three hours later I slipped into my bivvy bag behind a strand of trees next to some open ground on the edge of Hoyerswerda in Saxony. Things were good. My belly was packed with food from a nearby McDonald's and my saddlebag held a collection of their pastries and muffins that I would eat for breakfast. Above me the moonless night sky was filled with stars. I traced the faint edges of the Milky Way and picked out a few familiar constellations before drifting asleep in the humid night air.

Saddle Thor

It never always gets worse. But sometimes it gets worse for a long time.

The challenges were still piling up, and each day was proving more extreme than the last. I was managing to remain in good spirits most of the time, but this was the cheer of somebody getting satisfaction from dealing with adversity more than the happiness of somebody simply enjoying a bike ride. Each day, and each hour within each day, saw greater swings in my mood than the day or the hour before. The highs were getting higher, but the lows were also diving deeper.

My first task in Germany was to ride across the width of southern Saxony – a distance of around 240 kilometres. By now, the heat seemed solid, a vast club that threatened to knock me down whenever I stopped. This heat would remain with me throughout the remainder of my ride and I would spend the next week being drawn to any small scrap of shade like some sort of photophobic moth. That morning in eastern Germany the temperature quickly climbed to over 40 Celsius, peaking at 43. The wind was stronger and as contrary as ever and then, to complete the mix, I found a new challenge with the hills.

My route across Europe was as flat as I could reasonably make it, but the only feasible path across Saxony went right against the grain of the land, climbing from one river valley to another. I almost felt betrayed, as if I expected better from my old homeland. I had lived here in Saxony twenty years earlier, working in a brain-scanning unit in Leipzig where I ate my lunches in a hospital canteen full of patients who had pieces of their heads missing. The landscape around Leipzig had been unremittingly flat, almost like a part of the Netherlands, and I had forgotten that the rest of Saxony is much hillier. This particular part held a series of savage climbs over the foothills of the Elbe mountains, surrounded by endless fields of ripe brown wheat and young, bottle-green maize. These climbs had no carefully graded Alpine roads: they were up-on-the-pedals 15% lung-busting ascents. It was all quite trying.

But there was a big unexpected delight that day.

I had been on the road for about three hours when I stopped at a petrol station in Meissen for my first break of the day. Three hours was shorter than I would prefer for a block of riding but, travelling without a support crew, I had to adapt to where the facilities were. Even early in the morning, the cool air conditioning inside the petrol station was a pleasure. I pressed one cold drink to the back of my neck as I sipped another, watching the locals go about their morning routines. All the other customers seemed oddly relaxed and slow, and I had to check my phone before I realised it was a Sunday.

Twenty-five minutes after arriving, I wiped the last crumbs of pastry from my mouth with the back of my hand and headed out to the bike. Coming from the cool interior, the heat outdoors felt like walking into a wall. It was barely 0900 – what was this going to be like in the afternoon? I remounted the bike and headed through the rest of the city to begin a long steady climb to Nossen, the next town down the road.

I crossed the river and began to push up the slope ahead. As I followed a gentle bend around to the left, I spotted a figure dressed in white waving from a bus shelter. I had a moment of confusion: why would somebody be waving to me here? For a few seconds my legs continued to spin up the hill, mechanically pressing on with their routine as my mind struggled to catch up.

Standing in the bus shelter was Aleš Zavoral – Thor himself – the runner-up in the North Cape 4000 and my overnight companion in that Polish gold-lamé motel the previous year. I hurriedly pulled to the edge of the road and unclipped from my pedals. 'What...? You...?' I said eloquently.

'I came out from Prague to see you!' said Aleš, gesturing to his lovely 3T bike leant against a nearby wall. I was dumbfounded. He had followed me on the satellite tracker and arranged this surprise visit. He was on a 350-kilometre round-trip with no certainty that he would even find me. What a great guy. We hugged – perhaps with more enthusiasm from me than him, given my sweaty state – and then got back on the road, side-by-side.

Having company after all this time felt strange, and I was very aware of how much fresher Aleš's legs were than mine. It was clear he was having to hold back on the climbs whereas I, by now, was pressing on with the single power-level I had remaining to me. I could not help wondering what Aleš must be thinking about me. 'Is this all he's able to do?' he was surely thinking. 'How does he think he'll break a world record at this pace?'

Although it seemed almost impossible, the temperature continued to rise. My jersey was crusted white with salt and over the next hours Aleš and I performed a series of smash-and-grab raids on petrol stations for cold drinks and ice creams. I fell back into a pattern I first began on the Transcontinental Race: I always bought two ice creams so I could stuff the second down the back of my jersey while I ate the first. On one of these quick shopping stops I thoughtlessly bought a bar of white chocolate and slipped it into my handlebar food bag. Within minutes it was reduced to a sloshing packet of liquid. I bit the corner off the packet and squeezed the sweet claggy goo into my mouth.

I was flattered and pleased that Aleš had made the effort to come out and see me, but after ten days alone, wrapped in the intense focus of race effort, I was finding it hard to make conversation. My experiences, interests and concerns had been reduced down to water, food, shade and forward progress, and so I was content to let Aleš do most of the talking. But it was a pleasure to have him there. It seemed all too soon before we pulled up at an anonymous junction northwest of Chemnitz and said our goodbyes so he could head left and I could head right. I was so used to being focused in the moment that after only four hours of Aleš's company, it had become the new normal. For the first few minutes after he left, I kept checking over my shoulder, expecting to find him there.

The hills continued, each hard fought and won through the punishing super-heated air. I passed straight through Zwickau, Reichenbach and Plauen and saw the landscape begin to become less agricultural and more scenic – a small reward for all my labours. As I crouched into the headwind and grovelled up the ceaseless climbs I began to think about logistics. The ride had begun so well, with my 'start early-leave early' approach, but since the south of Finland my schedule had been slipping by about an hour each day. Yes, I had indulged myself with a couple of breakfasts in petrol stations to save morale, but the bulk of my lost time was thanks to winds, punctures and computer crashes – things outside my control. Still... those early starts and early finishes had been so incredibly convenient for finding food and for giving myself several hours each morning on silent, empty roads. There had to be some way I could get back into that routine. *Hmm...* I began to ponder.

At around seven in the evening I crested the highest point of the day at 530 metres and so crossed the boundary from

Saxony into the huge state of Bavaria. Entering this new *Land*, I made a decision: I would cut short this day and get myself back onto the proper schedule. This was a hard choice to make. To stop for the night after only 11 or 12 hours of motion was so far from my plan that I was almost offended by the thought. By now, my mind was firmly split into its two racing parts: the calm, rational mind and the fretting mind that took care of my progress beneath the surface, constantly policing me against anything that might feel like slacking. In the face of my ingrained need to keep pressing on, it took a special effort from my conscious mind to reassure myself that nothing was being lost. I had to re-mind myself that the clock forms a circle, and I was merely moving my overnight rest forward, not skipping any riding.

And so I dropped down into a town called Hof after 245 kilometres of grinding into the headwinds where, weaving around some half-finished roadworks, I found a hotel in the heart of the town. Here was my first chance to take advant-age of stopping early: I would buy the next morning's food ready for an early start the next day, just like I had during the first few days of this ride. But despite being only early in the evening, the receptionist told me there were no shops open at that time on a Sunday. 'Not in Hof!' she snorted, waving a dismissive hand in the direction of her sleepy little town.

This was a problem. If I left Hof early in the morning, I knew I would not reach another place to buy food for at least a hundred kilometres. I absolutely needed several hours' worth of food before I could think about leaving here. 'Can I buy some food from you?' I asked.

'*Ja*, the restaurant is open for another 30 minutes if you are quick,' she said.

'Great, yes, I'll eat there now. But I need food for tomor-row as well.'

She looked at me curiously, frowning. 'Breakfast is served from seven,' she said after a moment.

'Ah, no – I'll be leaving at about two o'clock in the morning. I won't be here for breakfast. I need breakfast I can take with me.' She shook her head, confused, and a long moment passed. I made things more concrete: 'Can you sell me some sandwiches?'

And so, as I left Hof at 0230 the next morning and began to pedal uphill through the pleasing chill of the night air, my saddlebag sagged beneath a fat cluster of cheese sandwiches prepared by the hotel chef. Thank goodness I spoke enough German to negotiate all that.

Screaming at the wind

Through the screams, the next day saw the best of me rise to the surface.

I had a few hours of peace before dawn. Winds in Europe are usually calmer during darkness, and the air was relatively still for a short time. Three hours after leaving Hof I was cruising through the sleeping streets of Bayreuth in the dark. The scenes here were familiar: my father and I spent a week together in Bayreuth for the Wagner festival a couple of years earlier; it was a pleasure to recognise landmarks we had visited together, and so think about him. But my respite from the wind was brief. Another hour down the road, as the sun erupted over the horizon, the gales returned. This being Germany, every town had a string of car dealerships on its outskirts and these served as regular reminders of my condition: each dealership had a string of flags outside, and I watched the thin ends of these thrash towards my face as I passed. Then, almost impossibly, as the morning progressed the wind somehow became even more brutal than before.

There is a service called MyWindsock, which uses weather data and GPS records from cycle computers to analyse past rides and work out the effects of the wind. I checked as I wrote this, and MyWindsock tells me that the day from Hof was the toughest headwind I have ever ridden into. I can believe it: there were times that day when the ceaseless resistance almost became too much for me. More than once I considered stopping and surrendering to the endless battering. I thought how wonderful it would feel to climb off my bike, lie down at the side of the road and just sleep forever beneath the shimmering cover of a poplar tree. There were moments when I threw back my head and screamed at the wind in frustration. But despite everything that wind threw at me, I continued to make painful progress into its face.

Loaded with my cache of cheese sandwiches, I was able to ride almost ten hours before taking my first proper break. They were ten gruelling, attritional hours, and I rode at an average speed of 22.1 kilometres per hour – far below what I would expect in still conditions – but I buckled down and did them anyway. There was screaming at the wind, and there was reminding myself it could never always get worse, and there was making videos for social media in which I tried to make jokes about my trials, and then there was shutting down my horizons to the next tree and riding only as far as that... I used one coping tactic after another, switching through my arsenal of techniques whenever necessary, as long as I just kept moving forwards. When focusing on the next tree stopped working, I started to think about all the people who knew I was doing this ride, and how hard it would be to explain to them if I stopped. I thought about how if I quit, I would just have to come back and do this all again next year, which would make all my efforts to date a waste. I thought about all the people who had encouraged and helped me get here. All these things kept me moving into the face of that wind.

That day in Germany, I really discovered how much I wanted to break this record.

To be clear, I do not think I was special in showing this resilience in the face of difficulty. I was not unusual because I completed this journey; if I did anything out of the ordinary, it was taking the first small steps that started me down the road. From there, the rest of the journey was made possible by properties common to us all. I started small and built upwards to bigger challenges, gaining confidence in the process – and we are all capable of that. I deliberately tried to learn and improve from every challenge I undertook. Again, we can all do that. I wanted it badly. Well, we all want things.

So the real question is whether I have anything that is *not* common? Is there something about me that means I can push through a daunting physical and mental challenge but you cannot? Perhaps – but more likely perhaps not. Sure, I enjoy the support of friends and loved ones who show confidence in me and who encourage me when I try to challenge myself, and not everybody has these. And before this, I had supportive parents who always made it clear that whatever I chose to do with myself was alright with them. Again, not everybody has these. But I am not sure that these things alone can explain why I am willing to attempt tasks that scare and excite me, and to keep on moving when these challenges prove so hard.

All I am saying is that if you have been holding back from pushing yourself to see what you are capable of, there is probably less reason for this than you think. Do not look at me, or people like me, and think we are different to you.

oOo

"What – you *don't* stay in five-star accommodation when you go bikepacking?"

I looked up into the camera, my expensively shampooed hair resting on a plush Egyptian-cotton pillowcase. The day was over: 367 kilometres completed after sixteen hours of slow, attritional grinding into gales.

"I've inadvertently booked myself into a five-star hotel in Germany, led astray by the fact it was really quite cheap. I've paid more or less this price for really foul accommodation in Britain. I think I'm going to stay exclusively in Germany from now on."

Crumbs, this place was nice. I regretted the fact I would be leaving so soon. I had booked the hotel online a couple of hours before reaching Ettlingen, right over in the industrial heartlands in the west of Germany, and had clearly got some sort of last-minute bargain. Rolling up amidst the sports cars and palm trees outside the entrance just as the sun began to set, I had decided I should brazen it out: I nodded confidently to the doorman and carried my bike through the marble reception area and up to the counter as though I did this every day. I was remembering my key bikepacking lesson for hotels: *Carry, don't roll.* But I needn't have worried here about being forced to store my bike in some insecure outdoor location. 'Would you like to keep your bike in the ballroom?' asked the friendly receptionist. 'It'll be quite safe there until morning – I can watch it all night.'

I asked if I could eat. The receptionist dinged a bell and at once a bustling pair of waiters appeared and smoothly escorted me to a large courtyard filled with dining tables. A fountain tinkled soothingly in one corner, soft music played, exotic plants swayed in a cooling summer zephyr. Despite my filthy sweat-streaked lycra, the waiters placed me exactly in the centre of the courtyard in full view of everybody present. I noted how all the other diners had chosen suits and smart dresses rather than skin-tight shorts smeared with food and snot.

I gobbled my dinner, then sluiced myself clean in my marble shower and climbed into bed to make a short video update before trying to get to sleep. I had a lot to look forward to that night. I was within striking distance of the

French border and, best of all, the weather forecast suggested that the wind would finally swing round to the north a
little the next day. I would believe it when I saw it, I
thought, but even the hint of a drop in the headwinds was
enough to make me more optimistic. I finished off my
video diary with thoughts about how my fretting mind was
starting to make itself felt the longer I had to rely on my
own resources:

> "The thing that's come to mind in the last couple
> of days is just how much additional work there is
> in doing a trip like this unsupported. I've always
> raced unsupported in the past, and so this is what
> I know, but it was just very interesting as I've
> come to the end of today – and the end of yester-
> day and the day before – to see the worry that
> starts to appear at four o'clock: *where am I going to
> end the day? How can I make sure I've got food?* and
> so on and so on. And then I started thinking*: ima-
> gine what that would be like if I had a support crew.*
> That contrast really came home to me and... yeah,
> basically it does feel like this is playing the game
> on hard level. Which is... good? Yeah, perhaps
> good later. But not so good today."

I uploaded the video and dropped instantly asleep.

Fighting fatigue

The ultradistance roller coaster sped on. For five days it had
been plunging down a slope, and I had needed to dig ever
deeper into my resources to complete the slow crawl across
Poland and Germany into the face of a punishing wind. But
that night, the turnabout finally arrived. The roller coaster
reached the bottom of the slope and, at last rounding the

nadir, began to climb up the other side. My first day in France was ridden on a high, my progress strong and in control once more. It was another reminder of the oldest lesson: keep on moving and everything comes good in the end. Just imagine if those five hard days had broken me, and I had given up before the upswing arrived. I shudder now at the thought of how easily that could have happened.

I retrieved my bike from the hotel ballroom and was on the road out of Ettlingen at around 0300. My legs were filled with a fresh vigour as I powered across the Rhine basin into France. Smooth straight highways slipped easily beneath my wheels and from my position down on the aerobars I turned my head to watch a soothing pink sunrise gradually fill the sky over the Black Forest. With exactly 2300 kilometres remaining to Tarifa, I crossed the Rhine into France after three hours' riding and began to pick my way through Strasbourg. It was a slow, fiddly affair of busy roads and twisting cyclepaths, but I had researched the route well, and it got me through the city as easily as could be expected for such a large conurbation. Four hours after setting off from my hotel, I was deep in the hills of the Vosges. Quaint villages full of half-timbered houses and steep church spires peeped coyly from within the pine forests that lined the valleys as I climbed up a nicely graded road to the 636-metre Col du Hantz.

The road surfaces had deteriorated notably as soon as I had left Germany, and I could tell these were slowing me down, but the wind had swung out of my face and for the first time in almost a week I did not feel constantly embattled. Riding the high after the roller coaster's upswing, I began to sing in the saddle.

oOo

'*Ça-va?*'

The words poked at the edges of my consciousness, but penetrated no further. I was dimly aware of being warm and dark and still. It felt good. But a moment later there was more sound – it was insistent, and was pulling me away from the cosy nest in which I was hiding. *'Monsieur? Ça-va bien?'* I opened my eyes and saw two women looking down at me. I glanced to either side and realised I had fallen asleep on a patch of ground outside a small-town super-market. 'I'm fine – thank you,' I reassured them, and then swore when I looked at the clock on my phone. Between the time spent shopping in the supermarket and the time lost accidentally falling asleep in this patch of shade, I had been here for over 45 minutes. I started to cram packets of food into my bags. I had to get back on the road. My legs turned slowly for the first kilometre, resentful about being dragged from that glorious rest.

I rode through a long picturesque slice of rural France on grippy, badly surfaced roads. In the afternoon I picked up the Saône river for a short distance before climbing up into more hills and boundless rolling fields. I cycled through a procession of small rustic towns, all of them sleepy and quaint: leathery farmers pottered around in rusty vans; old women walked purposefully through the streets with baguettes clutched beneath their arms. Between the towns, herds of mottled white cows slumped in whatever meagre shade they could find, their gaze slowly tracking me down the road as I passed.

If only I had the chance, I would cheerfully have emulated the cows and sagged in the shade. The sun continued to beat down, and any of its rays that missed on their first attempt bounced back at me from the hot roads. But despite this assault, I felt great that day. Freed from the constant resistance of the wind, my legs were back on form. I waved to the cows and turned the pedals, pulling into cemeteries for quick fill-ups whenever I needed more water.

My route planning for this trip had been meticulous. I had researched every possible food stop in detail and had a long list of options on my bike computer, often with their opening hours carefully noted. A typical entry might read 'Supermarket 06-20 (09-18 Sun)' or something like that. Other important pieces of research were also noted: 'Petrol station 06-22 NO FOOD FOR 160 KM STOCK UP HERE'.

Early on that first evening in France, as the daylight was just beginning to take on the earliest amber hints of sunset, my planning let me down for the first time. I knew I was due to arrive at a supermarket in a small town called Saint-Julien early that evening. I estimated that I would arrive in the hour before the shop closed at 2000, allowing me to buy everything I needed for that night and the following morning. But when I arrived, I found the supermarket closed and deserted. The opening hours published online must have been entirely wrong. Shit – this had never happened before, and I was a long way from any other shops. I retraced my steps to a nearby pizza takeaway and bought the largest pizza they could sell me. I ate half there and strapped the rest on top of my saddlebag to provide supper and breakfast. I left Saint-Julien feeling I had dodged a bullet: I might have had to make a lengthy detour if that pizza place had not been there. I wasn't comfortable having been saved by luck. It shouldn't need to come to that.

Darkness began to fall. I skirted around the north of Dijon in the growing gloom before dropping down to the bank of the Ouche river. In the blackness of a rural French night, the Ouche was a barely sensed presence off to one side of the road. The warm humid air was filled with insects that swarmed around the village street-lamps and bumped off my helmet with audible *pok... pok...* sounds.

I was now twelve days into this venture, and the accumulated fatigue was starting to make itself felt. My accidental nap outside the supermarket had been a sudden, deep sleep, but it had not been enough to catch up with all the rest that

I needed and I was aware of the fatigue building within me. It caught me by surprise again that evening. I rode along the river intending to press on into the night to try to get over the magic 400-kilometre mark, even though this would take me past the 16 hours of riding I aimed for each day. But then, abruptly, with ten kilometres left to reach this target, I was overwhelmed with a deep and pervasive weariness that came out of nowhere. There was none of the slow decline I would expect at the end of a day. Instead, my speed simply plummeted, all at once, as my body gave up.

Success depends upon our ability to learn from experience. And so, remembering my Operation Kickass days in the Transcontinental Race, I realised it would be a false economy to try to push through such powerful fatigue: riding when tired is just too slow to be worthwhile. The sensible thing is to stop at once and rest, and make back the time later. Without further thought, I swung the bike into a bus shelter on the edge of a small village and inflated my mattress. Chewing some more of my leftover pizza, I climbed into my bivvy bag and was asleep within minutes amongst a drift of dry fallen leaves on the cold concrete floor.

Freedom from choice

My North Cape to Tarifa record attempt was a nearly continual period of action and commitment. If a genie had transported you to a random point by the roadside just in time to see me ride by, you would almost certainly have turned to the genie and said something like 'Wow, that guy was really going for it'. Certainly, riding long days for more than two weeks meant I had to hold back and ride at a level of effort that was indefinitely sustainable, but I would still have passed your randomly chosen point crouched low over the handlebars, an expression of determination on my face as though the finishing line were in the next town rather than thousands of kilometres down the road. I was committed like this almost the entire time.

My race focus sometimes had comic consequences. I began each day with the goal of getting up, making myself ready, checking the bike, eating breakfast and being back on the road all in under 30 minutes. Trying to cram so much activity into such a short period led to absurdities like eating breakfast while sitting on hotel toilets – a process I came to think of as my 'one in, one out' policy.

This drive towards constant forward motion was in many ways its own pleasure. The single-minded pursuit of a world-record time was like a form of meditation: intense focus on one simple goal freed my mind from all other concerns. But there was also a sort of pleasure in having this process interrupted from time to time. During the first few days, being made to stop at traffic lights or roadworks was infuriating. I suspect every red light in Finland saw me muttering 'Come on come on come on come on...'. But later, deep into the ride, I reflected on how it could be a relief to have my choices taken away in these moments. Naturally, I had the liberty to do whatever I wanted all of the time – nobody was forcing me to do this ride – but the paradox was that my freedom was inherently unfree. Because I had made the commitment with myself to ride this journey as fast as I possibly could, I had left myself with only one option all of the time: ride, fast. The occasions when I had this process interrupted were the only times I was released from the tyranny of my freedom, able to stop and look around without being forced to face forward once more by the all-consuming drive to *just keep moving*.

But here's the thing: stopping can easily become a habit. And the slow seduction of immobility ate away at the hours that next day.

I woke early in my bus shelter and washed the last of my pizza down with the last of my water, getting back on the road at 0420 to continue down the river. Seventy kilometres later I had the first of my many stops, losing fifty minutes waiting for the disappointing minimarket in Autun to open – an unavoidable waste of time, as there would be no more shops for hours.

As the day went on, further valuable riding time was snatched from me in big, unhelpful chunks: a stop to adjust the bike's gears; then waiting for my computer to recover from a crash; then being overwhelmed with fatigue and having to take an eight-minute nap; then repairing a puncture; then stopping for food but finding the village shop so badly stocked that I had to stop again at the next town... It was one thing after another, and I grew frustrated at feeling so much time dribbling between my grasping fingers. Unlike some other days where I only realised I had wasted time later on, that day I was entirely aware of the problem at the time. When I uploaded my ride to Strava that evening, I titled it 'Get it together, Walker'.

The Fall and Rise

It is not just the mind that rides the ultradistance roller coaster. When pushed for weeks, the body has a separate up-and-down experience of its own. Perhaps the greatest success will one day go to the person who best understands the interplay and synchronicity of the two.

Where the body and mind differ, of course, is that the body is much easier to measure. So let's very briefly talk about some sports science.

Cyclists obsess about a number called Functional Threshold Power, or FTP. This is the measure, in Watts, of how much power you can squeeze into the pedals if you ride flat-out for roughly an hour. Without going into detail, the power output that you can produce for this length of time says a lot about your body's ability to supply energy to your muscles, which is why there is so much focus on this one-hour value. Measuring FTP is pretty simple: the best way is to ride flat-out for 60 minutes and see what your average power was afterwards. If you rode as hard as possible for an hour and did this at an average power of 220 Watts, your FTP would be something close to 220.

Another measure that cyclists spend a lot of time thinking about is ride intensity. This is the average power you sustained during a ride, divided by your FTP. In other words, it is a measure of how hard you pushed on a given ride relative to how hard you are capable of pushing for an hour. A big part of being a good cyclist, especially for solo efforts like time trials, is judging the intensity you can manage for whatever ride you are planning. This is the geeky heart of pacing strategy.

The reason it all becomes quite interesting and challenging is that the intensity you can sustain does not go up or down in a simple way as your rides get longer or shorter. Clearly you can ride harder for thirty minutes than you can for one hour. But while you might naively expect that a half-hour ride uses twice the power of a one-hour ride, it is not this simple. In reality, if you rode as hard as possible for thirty minutes you might only be able to generate 10% more power than you could manage for sixty minutes. Conversely, if you went for a two-hour ride, you would be going painfully slowly if you did this at half the intensity of a one-hour ride; it is more likely you would ride for two hours at around 85% of your one-hour power.

I can happily ride for six hours at 80% of what I can do for an hour. I can ride for sixteen hours at over 70% of my one-hour effort, although I might choose to rein that back slightly and be more conservative if I knew I was going to do the same thing the following day. Accordingly, I did my 1200-kilometre Easter training ride, which involved 48 hours of riding over three days, at slightly more than 60% of the intensity I can sustain for one hour. (One of the main reasons big rides are less intense than short rides is that I will take it easier on the climbs if I know I have to keep going for a long time.)

How does all this scale up to a ride that lasts for over two weeks?

Although I had a power meter on the bike, I rode across Europe largely by feel. I constantly asked myself 'Does the way I am riding seem sustainable? Could I do this indefinitely?' If I felt I was going too hard, I backed off; if I felt I could afford to push harder, I did so. On the road, how I was feeling was far more important than the numbers on my computer. But the data I recorded from my power meter became interesting once the ride was done.

These records show how my body changed and responded over the ride. The first seven days showed a steady decline in performance: even though the physical work *felt* largely the same from one day to the next, the power I was producing dropped off as fatigue kicked in. Day one saw me riding at 65% of my one-hour ability, Day Two saw me at 60% and by Day Four I was down to 53%. I hit the low point on Day Seven, when I was only able to produce 46% of my one-hour effort.

But then, on the eighth day – my first full day in Poland – a turnaround took place. The power I could produce jumped back up again, and from there, it continued to creep up from one day to the next. The final day of my record attempt would see me riding even more strongly than I had on Day Three!

There are not many sports where it takes a week to warm up.

The upswing in my body's performance after the first week is abrupt and obvious when looking at the numbers. But what is more interesting is that I felt the change at the time. Even as I was grinding into those unrelenting headwinds across Poland and Germany, I could tell that something was changing in my body. My strength, which had initially faded as the trip got underway, was slowly returning. I felt this particularly on Day Twelve, when I entered France and found my legs filled with a fresh fire that surprised me even at the time.

I had expected this ride to be one long, slow decline. This growing performance that took place over the second half of my journey was both unanticipated and necessary. Spain was approaching. It was time to climb.

Time to climb

I was on the road long before dawn, feeling like a burglar as I left a cheap, impersonal hotel in Limoges and slunk alone through the dark streets of the city. The early start gave me some relief from the heat and I resolved to make the most of it, putting in a solid stint of five and a half hours before taking my first break of the day. I thought of this as 'making hay while the sun didn't shine'.

When the sun finally appeared, I discovered that I had passed into wine-making territory without noticing the transition. The cows of yesterday were gone, and in the night I had been stealthily surrounded by endless rows of vines, their leaves rippling in the wind as I rode by. Just after midday I hit a further big landmark when I reached the Dordogne river. Less than a day earlier I had ridden over the Loire, and the day before that I had crossed the Rhine – this all helped me feel I was making solid progress across France. The sunlight shimmered blindingly on the waters of the Dordogne as I stopped next to the bridge for a confessional video diary entry about how I was finding the process of crossing France.

> "It's been relatively slow progress. The whole trip at the moment is on these small country lanes which have got really grippy, awful chip-and-seal surfaces. There's no expense incurred here on a good surface – they just go for whatever's cheap. So it feels slow and lumpy and I'm just grinding it out at a worse pace than I'd hoped for. But that's

alright – it is what it is, and I can almost smell Spain now, which is getting quite exciting.

"I was thinking, at the end of yesterday's ride, about how this experience of doing the record attempt differs from the races I've done in the past. Because, of course, with a race you can see where everyone else is and it's your position relative to everyone else that helps you make decisions about your pace. Whereas doing this thing that's just me is a really different experience. And in some respects it's a lot more stressful because it's kind of like there's two of me. There's the me that's out there flogging myself up hills and baking in 36-degree temperatures like this... and that's fine, I can handle that. The problem is, it's like there's another me over my shoulder, who's forever going 'Come on, let's be faster! Let's be faster! Are you sure you should be stopping? Do you really need to sit down? *Could you be putting those contact lenses in while you're riding?!'*

"I've got to say, I'm going to be very glad to get to the bottom of Spain and not have to listen to that guy any more, because he's getting to be quite hard work..."

oOo

When planning my route, I sought out roads that ran parallel to motorways. Motorways are expensive, so they are built as direct and as flat as possible. This meant that any road that followed one should also be direct and flat. It should be quiet too, because why would anybody drive on a smaller, slower road if there is a motorway right next door?

This tactic was a huge success. It meant that, as dusk approached on my last full day in France, I joined a road that hugged the edge of the A63 motorway for over 70 kilometres as it ploughed south across the western edge of the country. It was a curiously well-built service road, and was as quiet and as direct as I had hoped. I put in some easy distance as the whooshing traffic flashed by behind the barriers to my left, standing up on the pedals from time to time to relieve the growing pressure I was feeling from my saddle.

By now, I had been forbidding myself all thoughts of Tarifa for so long that it had become a habit. The end-point of this ride was so distant that to think about the gulf between here and there even for a moment was counterproductive. Whatever stage of the ride I was at, it was always true that anything could go wrong before the finish. I was haunted by the thought of a crack appearing my frame. I knew people who had experienced this, so it felt like a real and imminent risk – one that could take whole days to rectify. For this reason, I could never allow myself to think I had any sort of cushion against the current record.

But although the finish was still out of bounds, I did eventually allow myself to think about the beginning of the end. The Spanish border would be my last major landmark, introducing the final 1200 kilometres of riding. When planning my journey I had spent a lot of time looking for the best route across the Pyrenees and had settled on where the mountains hit the coast near Biarritz. I did not aim for the coast simply because it was the lowest point in the mountains – there is no flat route around the edge of Pyrenees because they merge straight into the Picos de Europa – but heading to the coast happened to access a useful road that would get me to the other side of the mountains with just 500 metres of ascent.

I slept on the ground behind a tennis club in a small village and then, in the cool air of the new morning, pressed through the darkness to the sea. After about an hour there was an abrupt change in the atmosphere as I hit warm breezes blowing in from the Bay of Biscay. These seemed to promise exciting new beginnings as they rustled the palm trees that lined the road. In the darkness, I passed through

Bayonne, Biarritz and finally Saint Jean de Luz. Then, as the sun erupted over the horizon to glitter upon the placid ocean, I started to attack a series of rolling headlands along the coast. Despite more than 5000 kilometres of accumulated fatigue and despite my short sleep, my legs felt strong on the climbs that day. My body was still on its upswing, and I found I could put down some good power on the punchy little ascents. I began to feel optimistic about the much larger climbs ahead of me in Spain, easily the hilliest part of the entire trip.

There was no gentle introduction to my final country. Lush green mountains swarmed around me as if from nowhere the moment I crossed the border and right away it was time to climb. I dropped into a comfortable low gear and ascended to Zamarraga at a good pace up a curving, graceful road. Initially the route took me through a series of factories and warehouses, but eventually I climbed out of the greys of humanity and into the soothing greens of nature. As the sinuous road brought me to the top of the ascent, with immaculate timing, *Let it Be* by the Beatles began to play in my earphones as the trees parted to reveal the encircling mountains and the green fields nestled in the valley below. The perfect coming together of music and landscape sent tears of emotion rolling down my cheeks as I crested the pass beneath the searing sun. Overwhelmed with the joy of cycling, I once again had that recurrent thought: *What if I had never dared to do this?*

Stay flexible

I *tap-tapped* the phone on my handlebars as I pedalled the bike through scrubby brown grasslands. *Hmm*, I thought, weighing up my options. I was soon going to drop into the ancient pilgrim city of Burgos, and I knew from my research that there was nothing at all for at least 130 kilo-

metres after I left there. From Burgos, my route took me
across the baked plain known as the *Meseta*, spoken of in
feared whispers for centuries by pilgrims on their way to
see the bones of Saint James at Compostela. There has
never been anything out on the *Meseta* for travellers. Even
today, there is only the skimpiest scattering of isolated
farming hamlets.

The problem was not the *Meseta* itself: it would be easy to
carry enough food and water to get me to the other side.
The real problem was that towns were going to be rare even
once I got through the plains. In this part of Spain, even the
populated areas have hardly anybody in them. I reckoned
that, if I passed through Burgos and rode into the night, it
might easily be ten or twelve hours before I found a food
shop that would definitely be open. I would hit the next
town – Valladolid, 155 kilometres away – at around 4 in the
morning, which would be too early. After this was Medina
del Campo, which I would reach at around 6. There *might*
be an early morning baker's shop open at that time, but
how confident did I feel about that in the middle of sleepy
rural Spain on a weekend? If I gambled on this and was
wrong, I would either have to wait around in Medina – perhaps for hours – until a shop opened, or press on another 55
kilometres to the next town, Peñarada de Bracamonte. The
only thing marked on my route sheet for Peñarada was a
hotel; there were no shops there – or, at least, none close
enough to my route for me to have flagged them up during
my planning. This all meant it would be 283 kilometres until I hit the first food shop that was definitely on my route
and definitely open: a petrol station one hour south of
Peñarada, which I knew from my research opened at 0800.

This all just felt too risky.

There is no victory in sticking to a plan in the face of
changing circumstances. I decided to finish this leg in Burgos, after just over 300 kilometres, and compensate by
shifting my day around once again to head out very early
the next morning. I was struck by the shift that had taken

place in my expectations. Two years earlier, riding my bike for 300 kilometres seemed like a massive undertaking, yet now 300 kilometres meant cutting the day short. How our horizons shrink when we stride towards them.

I made the decision to stop in Burgos just where the road crested the highest point of the day at 1000 metres altitude. I had reached this spot after a gradual 150-kilometre climb whose grinding ascent had been even more taxing than getting over the Pyrenees. Sitting on this peak in the road was a lonely, dusty petrol station, and I used it as a chance to stock up with several packets of sandwiches, breakfast and snacks for the next day, and a massive chocolate Swiss roll that promised to deliver more than 1200 calories for one Euro. The food was grim crap again, and I could surely have found something better in the city, but this roadside shop was definitely going to be quicker than searching the city streets and so the junk food won out. I was pushing for a world record, so the ticking clock was always the master.

The constant need to eat felt like a chore, and by this stage I was thoroughly bored with the whole process of putting food into my mouth. I would cheerfully have got all my energy from an intravenous drip if that had been an option. To stay on top of the physical effort, I was consuming between 8000 and 10,000 calories each day. As well as having to find and buy that sheer quantity of food, there was also a need to be disciplined and sensible about when I ate it. In particular, I knew from hard experience that it was essential to have a good feed before going to sleep: although it was always tempting to give in to the fatigue and go straight to sleep after a hard ride, skimping on the last meal of the day would leave me weak and sluggish in the morning. Like skipping sleep, skipping a big evening feed was a false economy when playing a long game like this.

That night in Burgos was easily the lowest point in my long string of necessary evening meals. I checked into a hotel, had a very quick shower and was all set to climb into bed within minutes of reaching my room. After another hot, gritty day of riding, that bed was calling to me with a siren song of clean sheets and sleep. But I knew I couldn't allow myself to submit to its embrace until I had swallowed a couple of thousand calories. Always aware of time passing, I had to do this quickly. With grim determination I ripped open two packets of tuna sandwiches and ate these in a few bites. Then, with all the enthusiasm of somebody about to remove their own eyelids, I tipped back my head and lowered the entire Swiss roll down my throat in one long motion.

Bookends for the day

I was back on the road before three o'clock, heading out into a long morning of superlatives. I left Burgos under the clearest, darkest night sky I had ever ridden beneath. The moon had chased the sun over the horizon hours ago, and it was only a few minutes before I reached the edge of the city and passed the last of the streetlamps. Leaving this final pool of artificial light and heading into the void beyond felt like casting off from land and sailing out into a vast uncertain ocean. The darkness here on the *Meseta* felt tangible; it was hard to believe this was the mere absence of light. It took courage to head out into such erasing blankness.

But what rewards I got! As the city glow receded behind me and my eyes adjusted, I found diamond-sharp stars so numerous and bright that the familiar constellations were difficult to find amongst their clutter. The Milky Way was instantly visible overhead, stretching from one horizon to the other. From time to time I stopped on the road, turned off my headlamp and took a moment to stare in awe at the wonder of our galaxy. For this spectacle, I was willing to add a few minutes to my record attempt.

I pedalled on through the darkness. The plain here was as empty as I had thought it would be, and I had been right to be cautious about what time of day I tackled it. For hours I saw nothing except a couple of tiny farming villages, shuttered and still as they clung tightly to the road for protection against the night. I stopped in the centre of one of these villages to eat a quick meal by an old water pump. It felt strange to sit there, my presence entirely unsuspected by the sleeping villagers in their dusty houses. Once again I felt like an intruder, slipping through the lives of thousands of people right across this vast continent.

Time moves differently when we should be asleep, and so it seemed a long time until sublime night gave way to perfect dawn. Its appearance was at first almost imperceptible, and if it had been later in the year I would have assumed I was detecting the false dawn of zodiacal light. But here, in the middle of summer, this was the real thing – just tantalisingly slow in its appearance. As I followed the oval beam of my headlamp down gentle slopes amidst unseen fields of wheat, I sensed the first tentative prick of light in the east. It was so faint that, for a moment, I thought I must be seeing the glow of a solitary streetlamp in a distant hamlet. The sun responded to my doubts by dramatically ripping apart the black curtains that had sat across the horizon. Over the coming half-hour, I was treated to the most stunning sunrise of my life. The fresh life it threw across the land was all the more intense in contrast with the darkness it replaced. I paused by the roadside to eat breakfast, and watched sunlight pour like honey over the ridges and furrows of the land.

oOo

Somewhere south of Salamanca I crossed a dam at the end of a vast reservoir and there picked up a long stretch of old main road that had been superseded by a motorway. This road ran for hundreds of kilometres, all the way to Seville, and had called to me from the map when I was doing my

route planning. Working on the computer at my kitchen
table earlier that year, I had dropped the Google Streetview
marker onto this road over and over all along its length.
Each time I had seen the same thing: a wide, smooth and
empty carriageway that cried out to be ridden. No matter
where I had looked at this road online, it seemed perfect,
but I still could not bring myself entirely to trust my research. Surely anything that looks too good to be true has to
be false?

It was as good as I hoped. Practically all the traffic was on
the parallel motorway, and I had this wide, high-quality
road almost to myself. For most of its length, resupply was
easy: the road took me through the centres of towns from
time to time; it was also easy to access motorway service
areas and their quick, simple shops and cafes. What a relief
it was to have the logistics of this ride made easy for a while,
especially when the pounding heat forced me to drink so
much.

The road headed upwards, taking me to the highest point
of the entire ride at the 1202-metre Puerto de Vallejera. I
swung away from the motorway slightly here – the old road
crawled around the rocks at the summit whereas the new
road had a flatter route blasted out of the mountain – but I
could still hear the sound of distant lorries labouring up the
slope on the other side of the hill. The noise reassured me
that the effort I was having to make up the final ascent was
not merely down to tired legs.

And then it was a downhill whoosh for two and a half
hours. The sun, which had treated me to that splendid dawn
a few hours ago, was heading for the opposite horizon and
casting long shadows across the swaying brown grasses as I
crested the pass. It soon disappeared in a final blaze of amber light as I dropped almost 900 metres down the other
side of the mountain. Once again I was in the darkness, but
this time a darkness of a more comforting, urban variety;
the air was close and humid as I rolled through dark streets.
I pressed on until shortly before midnight when, after 392

kilometres of riding, I rolled into a hotel on the edge of Plasencia.

Four hours later, long before the following dawn, I handed the key back to the same night manager who had checked me in. 'Is there a problem with the room?' he asked, his face full of polite concern. I smiled and got back on the road.

I was still not allowing myself to think about Tarifa; but now, for the first time, I did start to believe this ride might one day end. Up until this point, it had been imperative to live each day as though I would be doing this forever: I could not afford to skimp on food or sleep, nor to push as hard as I might like, because that might mean I could no longer churn out one solid day of riding after another. But here, as I reached the parts of Spain that lie south of Madrid, I permitted myself for the first time to understand that I would not ride indefinitely, and that I could begin at last to let myself go towards the final stretch. Deliberately cutting into my overnight rest was now feasible, and I was glad to do it.

The overwhelming richness of the ride

Ultradistance cycling distorts time and space.

If you spend a day driving, you travel a long way and see nothing. If you spend a day walking, you travel a short distance but, in compensation, you see every small detail along the way. The efficiency of the bicycle gives you the best of both modes. On a bike, you can travel a long way *and* see a huge amount. The cyclist experiences both breadth and depth.

On a one-hundred kilometre ride, it is pleasing to see so many intricate details that you would otherwise have missed: a house with a mailbox the shape of a rampant dragon; a shop in a small village selling nothing but grey wooden horses. *How does that stay in business?* you wonder, before immediately being distracted by the next sight.

But when you step up to riding several hundred kilometres in a day, and doing this for more than one day, the richness of bicycle travel can almost become overwhelming. *Hey, remember that village square with all the mannequins hanging off the rooftops?* you idly muse. *When was that... four days ago? Five?* Then there is a weird moment of recalibration as you realise it was earlier that morning. The tumble of detailed experiences between now and then pushes back your recent experience until it feels like the distant past. Contemplating the huge number of scenes you remember witnessing that day, you start to worry about how many more you have already forgotten.

oOo

I crossed another dam, this time on the vast river Tajo, and pushed on south for seven hours through Cáceres and Mérida. The heat in central Spain was as punishing as ever, and climbed to 40 degrees again that day. But my legs were working for me, and I was handling the punchy little climbs far better than I would ever have imagined at this stage. On the way into Mérida I found myself in the middle of a Sunday club ride. The other cyclists looked the part – nice kit, expensive sunglasses, riding briskly on shiny road bikes with no luggage to slow them down. Despite my bags, and despite having almost 6000 kilometres in my legs, I put the hammer down and dropped the lot of them on a short climb on the way into the city. It was easily the smuggest thing I've ever done on a bike. I watched them recede behind me in my little rearview mirror, astonished at how my body was recovering more each day.

For the first time, the outside world gave hints that I might be approaching the end of Europe. I stopped for food at a motorway service area and noticed a booth selling ferry tickets from Spain to Morocco. Africa! The port was within a day's drive of here. It was also, for the more determined cyclist, within a day's ride.

There was one last real climb: an all-afternoon grind up a gradual slope to a sleepy, parched town called Monasterio. From here it was another downhill swoop to Seville, where I finally said goodbye to the parallel motorway that had guided me so well for the past two days. I was sorry to see it go.

That long climb produced some difficult moments where I was again having to dig down to keep myself in good spirits as I pushed on through the heat. I sat on the ground outside a petrol station just before Seville at nine o'clock that evening and summarised the challenges in the last of my video diary entries:

> "It's been a challenging afternoon. Same as yesterday, it got to ten or eleven o'clock and the temperature skyrocketed. Then *crazy* winds kicked in – really really strong and, worst of all, blustery and unpredictable. The kind of wind that's constantly throwing your front wheel around. It's been hard work.
>
> "But hey! The important point is, I'm 335 kilometres down for the day and it's only 208 to the finish. So... [a hint of a smile] obviously I'm going to push through the night. I think there's no question about this. It's only 208 kilometres. That's an audax, that's a randonnée. That's what we do on Sundays without thinking about it.
>
> "So I'm going to hit the road and blast through the night because, in a matter of hours, that world record could be mine."

It was the first time I had said it out loud.

The longest night

Large cities are never easy to cross. Even on a Sunday, and with most of the day finished, Seville did not want to let me go. Through the humid darkness of early evening, I surged from one slow red traffic light to the next, hopping from crowded main roads to useless off-road cycle paths according to whichever looked best at the time. Time dragged on; it felt as though I might never get out of this city. Might I be doomed to lurch from one red traffic light to another for eternity, like some sort of Flying Dutchman? The roads swarmed with frantically driven cars. The fury of the noise and motion was overwhelming after the peace of Spain's interior. There was no place for a lone long-distance cyclist in this neon maelstrom.

There was little comfort when I eventually got to the other side of the city and emerged into the night outside. I found myself with a nagging feeling of discomfort, as though I were waiting for something to go wrong but did not know what. Perhaps it was the novelty of riding into the night knowing that I was going to push right through to dawn; I hadn't yet done that on this trip. Or perhaps I felt uneasy at the faint thought that I might be about to lose the sense of purpose that had driven me this far. What would I do with myself when I no longer had to keep moving forward at all times?

The bike also seemed reluctant to press on into the warm sticky night beyond the city. I kept having to stop and fiddle with things: I stopped outside a huge darkened factory to replace the batteries in my backup rear light; I stopped again outside a sleeping school to tighten the battery cover on my power meter. I already knew I was riding slowly thanks to the fatigue, the darkness and the bad roads; all these delays felt like they were piling up on top and making me even slower.

That last night through the south of Spain was hard – really hard. Now I had finally let myself go for the final push to the finish, my body was in a slow spiral of collapse and it was only the force of my desire that was keeping me moving. I wanted so badly to get this done, but things kept happening to keep the finish out of my reach. I lost a big chunk of time after a fragment of fine wire embedded itself in my rear tyre, lodging deep within the rubber at a strange angle so that it punctured two replacement inner tubes before I was able to find it. It was the sort of taxing delay that I really did not want at that stage. The only good thing about the puncture was the offer of help from two passing police officers in their patrol car. 'No, no, *de nada*,' I reassured them. I wanted their help and their company, but seemed to fear breaking the solitude of my record attempt at this late stage.

Once the tyre was repaired, there were some horrible kilometres on a fast, crowded main road full of roadworks before I got out into more remote farmland. Then my computer crashed on the edge of a tiny village. Yet another fifteen minutes were lost waiting for it to reboot as I grew cold in the night air while an unseen chorus of furious dogs howled and barked at my presence.

I was crawling at a pathetic pace by now. As I had discovered back on the Transcontinental Cycle Race, pushing right through the night feels hardcore but is almost always a false economy. Although dawn brings fresh life, the hours running up to this reprieve see you grinding slowly to a halt as the fatigue builds. Wrapped in a jacket against the cold, I should have got into my bivvy bag and slept for an hour or two to hit my body's reset switch, but the idea that I might be able to get myself to the end with one last push of over 500 kilometres overwhelmed my rational mind. The need to get this ride finished had been tamped down for one day after another, and I could contain it no more. The road began to roll up and down a series of hills, slowing me further. By this point I was riding at less than 20 kilometres per hour. I was dragging myself forward like a wounded animal. I was a being comprised of pure will.

oOo

Ultradistance athletes talk about hallucinations a lot.

I first learned about this years earlier when I explored the Long Distance Walkers' Association and their annual hundred-mile walk. People who walked slower than average in this event, or people who lingered too long in the food stations during the first 36 hours, might find themselves having to walk right through a second night before completing their hundred miles. The second night was always spoken of with exaggerated respect by those who had walked through it. The second night was the tough one. It was the night where people dropped out despite being only eight miles from the finish. It was the night where people... *saw things*. Walkers talked about finding hotels full of watchful badgers, or seeing costumed dancers performing ballet at the side of the footpath.

I later found that these same kinds of spectacle were described by long-distance runners. The fatigued loneliness during the second night of the Ultra Tour du Mont Blanc led to some people seeing things; longer races like the Tour des Géants in Europe or the Tahoe 200 in the USA seemed to produce hallucinations in practically everybody. A few cyclists in the Transcontinental Cycle Race had talked about similar experiences, hopefully taking these as a sign that the time had come to get off the road for a lie-down.

Whether walking, running or cycling, I had never seen anything like this at all, and deep down I was always slightly disappointed. I have never had any interest in hallucinogenic drugs, perhaps because I have always been frightened by the idea of a bad trip. There was a phase of people experimenting with LSD and magic mushrooms at my school when I was around 18, and the stories that people told in the classrooms on Monday mornings put me off for life. But the experiences recounted by sleep-deprived long-distance athletes always seemed to be of a different sort to those teenage trips. I never heard a runner talk about seeing something frightening; the hallucinations were always described as feeling benign. The unexpected herd of rhinoceroses wants to show you the way, not trample you. The woman with the accordion who appears in the middle of the blizzard just really wants you to enjoy her song.

The closest I have ever come to any sort of hallucination was the tunnel vision I experienced that final night through the south of Spain. I did not see anything that was not there (as far as I know), but what did happen was that I was seized with a clear and irrational *certainty*. After two weeks of driving relentlessly towards Tarifa, and after pushing into the night after a long hot day of riding, I spent several hours on that final night convinced that my road ran along a narrow causeway that stretched between me and my goal in Tarifa. In reality, I was deep inland at this point, and there were vast reaches of dusty plain all around me, but at the time I was certain that the solid ground ended just a few hundred metres to my left and to my right, slightly beyond the mesmeric flashing lights of the wind farms that clustered near the road. For me, there was nothing but the turbines and the dark ribbon of road that ran between them towards the finish line. And over there beyond the turbines...? I didn't know. Ocean? Mist? Void? It didn't occur to me to think *what* might be there – I knew, as a certainty, there was nothing beyond, and that was all I needed to know.

And so, utterly fixated on what lay ahead at the end of this road, I crawled through the night.

oOo

At this point, being alone was a choice.

I have always been an independent person. While I would certainly not describe myself as antisocial or misanthropic, I am capable of being satisfied with my own company and of managing with my own resources. Perhaps this comes from being an only child. It is possible that I am good at undertaking these long-distance challenges because of this streak in my personality that lets me enjoy solitude without feeling deprived.

But, that said, being alone was a choice.

My partner, Louise, had arrived in Spain a day earlier along with her parents, my mother and my stepfather. They would be my welcoming committee when I finished this challenge. I had spoken to Louise early that evening as I negotiated my way through Seville, and then I spoke to her again around midnight. 'Do you want us to come out and see you?' she asked that second time. It was as if she sensed my downward spiral. At the time I had demurred, saying I would meet them at the finish line. I had set out on my own, and it seemed fitting that I would complete the entire ride alone, only reconnecting with people from my real life at the moment the journey was over. I somehow felt that would keep the record attempt special and pure – a life within a life.

But that dark night in the hills wore me down. All alone, crawling along an imaginary treadmill, I wanted the comfort of familiar faces. At 4 in the morning I called Louise. 'It would actually be really nice to see you,' I said. It was a difficult thing to admit after such a long spell of absolute self-sufficiency.

We arranged to rendezvous near Vejer de la Frontera, where the rural road I was following southwards would hit the final main road that was to sweep me down to Tarifa. It would take the best part of two hours for me to get to our meeting-place; through the darkness, this seemed the longest two hours of my life. Once I had broken the seal, and admitted the need to see familiar faces after these weeks of severe autonomy, the need for those faces ate away at me. My situation was not helped by running low on food – a stupid misjudgement that slowed my progress even further.

The blinking red lights of the wind farms still surrounded me. The turbines were scattered across a wide area, and it was almost unnerving to see their warning lights flashing in synchrony, given how far apart the masts stood. These wind farms were here for a reason: this region of Spain is forever windy, making the coast around Tarifa popular with windsurfers and kitesurfers. I had felt the winds building over the past couple of days as I had got closer, and their blustering and buffeting made that last night even more challenging. Abruptly, as huge blades thrashed the skies to either side of the road, I felt the wind veer from my face to hit me sideways. I canted over to my left to stop the gale from tipping me over, then laughed out loud when I realised that I was here in Spain, quite literally tilting at windmills.

These last hours were hard. They were also, now that I finally understood that I might reach the end, a time to reflect on the journey that had brought me here.

What a progression I had seen over the past three years.

First there had been the Transcontinental Cycle Race, entered on a whim with no experience or expectations – just a desire to see what would happen when I threw myself into some vast venture way beyond my previous experience and comfort. That race had shown me I was capable of riding long distances faster than I had ever dared to imagine. It threw up tantalising possibilities by suggesting that here was a sport that I might actually be quite good at.

Then there was the North Cape 4000, which woke within me a previously unsuspected urge to compete and win. What a revelation that had been, after a lifetime of never even suspecting I had such drives. How fascinating it was to finish first in that event and see what it was like to be the victor... even to be gently lionised for a short time (albeit in the extremely minor way afforded to winners in sports that nobody has ever heard of).

Both of these previous events had taught me valuable lessons – practical lessons, but also deeper, more personal lessons about who I was and what I could do. And so here I was on this culminating record attempt, pushing through the night, through the fatigue and the pressure sores as I attempted to convince myself that my winning ride the previous year had not just been a fluke...

Abruptly, I pulled off the road and, with a crunch of gravel, my headlamp swung around in a wide arc to reveal a set of blinking faces inside a parked car. Doors opened and my welcoming committee climbed out into the car park of a closed restaurant where we had arranged to meet. They offered hugs, greetings and, best of all, homemade cake. I didn't stay long – my tired body quickly felt the cold once I paused in my riding, but it was good to see them. 'I'll see you again in Tarifa,' I said, and headed back out into a darkness that was finally tinged with the first hints of a long-awaited dawn. Our meeting had reassured me that the end of this ride was both real and imminent.

I was on a main road now, but with my exhausted body and lack of sleep my pace was still poor. I was clearly aware how much I was fighting fatigue. At one point, shortly after the sun rose, I came the closest I have ever come to falling asleep on the bike. My head started to drop and I had to stop and sit down on the barrier at the side of the road for a moment for a microsleep. I rested for only a minute or two, and jerked back awake as soon as I began to nod off, but those brief seconds of sleep were enough to get me moving again. I remounted the bike and continued down the road. I was so close to the finish, but there was not yet any elation, or even relief. There was only the intense focus on dragging myself forward. I existed right behind my eyeballs, a glowing pinpoint of determination.

The violent headwind was growing with the daylight, and my speed was far too low. Seeing Louise and our parents had tricked me into feeling the ride was over. I almost began to regret cracking and meeting them before the finish. Seeing them was supposed to mean the ride was over and yet here I was, still crawling along this road into a gale. Why wasn't this ordeal complete? Why did I still have (a quick check of the computer – *shit!*) thirty-five kilometres to go?

Those last hours required as much resolve as any other stretch of the ride. The closeness of the finish line made the final kilometres all the more difficult. Crouched as low on the bars as my saddle-sore body would allow, I tried to distract myself, and when that didn't work, I tried to focus on how I would feel to break this record. Because now, finally, I could see that I would do this. For the first time, as Tarifa appeared ahead, I truly accepted that my goal could be reached.

Only then, once I finally believed I would finish, did my focus shift at last to the time. What exactly would the new record be? I turned off the main road and followed the arrows on my misbehaving cycle computer through the confusing twists and turns of Tarifa's streets. The ride officially ended on the causeway that ran from Tarifa to Isla de las Palomas, but a series of junctions, roundabouts and U-turns slowed my arrival. While scanning the streets for traffic, I was also switching my computer back and forth between the map and the screen that displayed the time. *Click* – the map... still on course. *Click* – sixteen days, twenty hours (*did I have that right? Had I correctly worked out the time zones? Yes, yes, I was sure I had*) and... fifty-nine minutes. Sixteen days, twenty hours and fifty-nine minutes. I turned a final corner and there, ahead of me, was the causeway, running away in a dead-straight line across the sea. In a final defiant burst of activity I hammered at the pedals as my face crumpled and I began to cry. 'Sixteen days, twenty hours and fifty-nine minutes,' I said out loud. 'I've done it. I've done it.' There was no sense of triumph, simply relief. I had set out to do something extremely difficult and I had done it. Nothing had gone wrong to stop me. I had risen to the challenge. At last, I could stop hurting myself.

My task complete, I climbed off the bike.

The End

With the record broken, I guess I can confess my secret ambition.

I told nobody about this before attempting my ride. My ambition was a little hidden extra, an additional challenge kept for myself alone. I only revealed it to Louise one or two days before the finish.

You might remember that the record for crossing Europe the other way – east to west – was broken the year before my ride by Leigh Timmis. Leigh crossed the continent with a support crew and managed an overall average of 370 kilometres per day.

My secret ambition was to ride faster than this *without* support. I felt that riding faster than the supported record would allow me to say, without qualification, that I was the fastest person to cross Europe on a bicycle.

Almost as soon as the ride was over, I tallied the numbers.

I had cycled across Europe, unsupported, at 377 kilometres per day.

Not bad for somebody who spent decades believing he was bad at sport.

Shortly after I finished my ride, while still in Spain, I got a message from James Hayden, once my most feared rival for this record:

"Mega ride. That'll stay for a while!"

Let's hope so.

This is not to say that I don't want other people to try and take this record from me. I hope people will. Indeed, I'm happy to help them if they ask. This is not so they can experience the pleasure of breaking the record (it's not a pleasure – it's a relief), but so they can experience the pleasure of training for it, and the sense of purpose that comes from devoting your life single-mindedly to a concrete goal for the long period of time required. These are the real rewards. It might not surprise you to learn that, once my world-record ride was complete, I spent some months feeling a little lost and adrift. I had been steering towards a fixed destination for so long that I had forgotten what it was like to live without that goal. It truly can be better to travel hopefully than to arrive.

At the risk of stating the obvious, breaking an ultradistance cycling world record was really very difficult. It took physical and, especially, mental reserves that I had never tapped into before. At the moment my ride ended and I dismounted from the bike, I felt I had given everything I could have given, which was exactly what I hoped I would feel. This was likely going to be the biggest, hardest challenge of my life, and it was fitting that I would squeeze everything out of myself in the process.

And yet...

In those first few days after my big ride was over, as I relaxed in Spain enjoying the pleasure of not needing to move anywhere and being able to eat fresh, sugar-free food, thoughts of what I had just done crowded and jostled in my mind. As I started the long process of sifting and making sense of the experience I had gone through, I found myself returning to one persistent thought, one clear and startling realisation that forced itself immovably into my mind:

I could have done that faster.

Let's never stop trying to improve.

The world record for cycling across Europe (North Cape to Tarifa, or vice-versa)

Year	Rider	Time
2011	Glen Burmeister	39 days, 11 hours, 24 minutes
2013	Paul Spencer	22 days, 11 hours, 28 minutes
2015	Lee Fancourt	21 days, 14 hours, 29 minutes
2019	Rob Gardiner	19 days, 11 hours, 5 minutes
2019	Ian Walker	16 days, 20 hours, 59 minutes
?	?	?

With thanks to @hugovk: https://twitter.com/hugovk/status/1146425230824542208

Afterword

Many people have remarked on how time makes us forget pain and suffering. Writing this book, I was able to see the process at work in myself. When I was writing the section about crossing Latvia during the world record attempt, for example, I originally started to write about how easily and quickly I went through the country on its high-quality highways. That was what I remembered when I sat down to write that section several months after the event. Then I rewatched the video diaries that I had kept at the time. I was startled to see how tired I looked as I slumped outside petrol stations cramming ice cream into my face. I heard myself talk about how difficult I was finding the roads, how slow my progress was and how low my mood had become. I didn't remember any of that! The negativity had been gently erased over the intervening months. It was fascinating to see this happen first-hand.

Speaking of negativity, I have still not quite got over my imposter syndrome. If winning an international contest and breaking a world record haven't fixed this, I'm not sure if anything will. There is a sense in which, intellectually, I know I am a relatively elite cyclist (I cringed as I typed that, and could not bring myself to edit out the qualifier), but I still do not really believe it emotionally. The only time the doubts disappear is when I am sat on the bike. And it only takes one bad training session for them to come back.

And so, of course, there were many times when I felt like a fraud writing this book. Although I have achieved some things on a bike, I am aware that I have been riding for far fewer years than a lot of other people. I often found myself thinking 'Who am I to be giving advice on this stuff?'

One of the reasons I carried on writing was that I am an academic. Thanks to years of training and experience, my instinct is always to induce: I automatically ask how my specific experiences might point towards some wider lesson. This ability to generalise is not something that comes naturally to everybody, and was a big reason I finished this book. While I hope you found my experiences interesting or entertaining, I hope much more that you found value in the lessons I drew from them.

The other thing that kept me writing was the discovery that people seemed genuinely to be inspired by the things I had done. Shortly after finishing my world record ride, I had various people tell me that they had recently taken up some new sporting activity specifically as a response to seeing what I did. One person joined a gym, another started running and entered a race... something she had wanted to try for a long time but had not dared. Somehow my doing this big ride was causing people to ask 'What will *I* do?'. This is easily the most rewarding aspect of breaking the record, and so this book, more than anything, is presented in the hope that more people will ask themselves those same questions:

What will *I* do?

When will I start to do it?

Thanks

I was afraid to write this section, because I was so worried I would miss somebody out. I was tempted to leave these pages out of the book altogether, thinking it better to offend everybody rather than somebody specific. But in the end, I felt I had to write it because although I was out there alone on each of those big rides, there was a bunch of people who had played a role in getting me get there and it would be disingenuous to imply I had done it all alone.

Obviously I should start with my parents, Janet and Stephen, without whom none of this would have been possible.

Then there is Louise, whose support and belief have made more difference than she can know. Thanks, Loulou.

Rick Barton casually invited me to enter a running race back in 2013 and pretty much changed my life.

My coach Holly Seear was a delight to work with, and could not have been more supportive in getting me to North Cape in the best possible shape to take on the record.

Several companies helped me out with equipment on the world record attempt, and I'm grateful to them for showing belief in me. Particular thanks to Apidura, Stayer Cycles and Veloskin.

Meg Whelan was kind enough to read the first draft of this manuscript and give me useful feedback.

Finally, I'd like to thank all the people who have kept me company on rides over the past few years. When I start to think of all the cyclists with whom I've shared several hours' riding and conversation on audax events, the number quickly becomes overwhelming and I could not begin to list them all. But there are a few fellow cyclists who made a more substantial difference in one way or another. So in no particular order, I'd like to thank the people who have been there for the really big stuff: Richard Coomer, Aleš Zavoral, Ian Garrard, Mark Townsend, Matt Jones, Alan Colville, Andy Gregg, Robert Wragge-Morley, Anthony Levy and all the riders at Audax Club Bristol with whom I don't ride as often as I'd like thanks to my training schedules.

Appendix – World record attempt kit list

A certain amount of this kit was insurance against the Arctic cold. I probably wouldn't take quite so much clothing, for example, if I were not going into cold regions; or I might omit the sleeping bag. But a painfully cold night in the Arctic during the North Cape 4000 race had left me nervous, so I erred on the side of caution as I ventured back into that region.

I know it might look like there were a lot of tools and spare parts – but most of these were tiny items and they all fitted into a small pouch.

- **Bike**
  - Whyte Wessex One (with a few modifications – most notably upgraded brakes, brake levers/gear shifters, bottom bracket, seat post and saddle). Garmin Vector 3 power-meter pedals.
- **Wheels**
  - Stayer 50 mm carbon rims, SON Precision dynamo hub (front) and Bitex hub (rear)
- **Tyres**
  - Continental GP5000 Tubeless (which ended up with tubes in for most of the ride)
- **Lights**
  - Busch & Müller IQ-X (front), Busch & Müller Mu (rear). Backup blinky rear light with AAA batteries

- **Power system**
  - Sinewave Revolution USB charger, connected to the dynamo.
- **Bags**
  - Apidura frame pack (used for things needed during the day), Apidura saddlebag (used for overnight items and things like spare parts that I would only need very occasionally), and Apidura top-tube pack (for small items)
- **Eating and drinking**
  - Morsel spork
  - 2 bidons
- **Sleeping**
  - Bivvy bag
  - ¾-length inflatable ultralight mattress
  - Lightweight down sleeping bag
- **Clothes**
  - Jersey
  - Bib-shorts x 2 (extravagant!)
  - Warm sleeveless undershirt
  - Pair of socks
  - Shoes
  - Helmet
  - Shoe covers
  - Thermal gilet
  - Windproof gilet
  - Arm warmers
  - Leg warmers
  - Buff
  - Waterproof jacket
  - Neoprene gloves
  - Hi-viz harness
- **Medical and toiletries**
  - Painkillers
  - Caffeine pills
  - Veloskin chamois cream
  - Lip balm

- Sun screen
- Sudocreme
- Razor
- Toothbrush and paste
- Contact lenses
- Wet wipes (to clean me and the bike)
- **Mechanical**
  - Pump and tiny spare pump
  - Tyre pressure gauge
  - Inner tubes x 3
  - Tyre boot
  - Spare tyre
  - Puncture patches
  - Spare tubeless valve
  - Valve extenders x 2
  - Spare valve core x 2
  - Valve core tool
  - Replacement disk brake pads x 4
  - Spare brake pad retaining bolt and clip
  - Lezyne multitool (provided all necessary allen keys, T10 Torx key, spoke keys and chain tool)
  - T20 torx key (for headlamp bracket)
  - Tyre levers
  - Chain lube
  - Quick-links to rejoin chain if it snapped
  - Zip ties
  - Spare gear inner cable
  - Spare mech hanger
  - Nitrile gloves
  - Folding emergency spoke
  - Strong tape (wrapped round pump)
- **Electronics**
  - Phone
  - Bike computer
  - Heart-rate monitor

- Spot tracker and a reuseable zip tie to fasten it to the saddlebag
- Spare batteries for the Spot tracker
- Spare batteries for the blinky lamp
- Spare battery for heart-rate monitor
- Spare batteries for my power meter
- 10,000 mAh rechargeable battery pack (charged during the day from the Sinewave charger and used to charge appliances at night)
- Spare headlamp (also doubled as a small extra battery pack)
- Multi USB mains charger
- USB cables to charge bike computer, phone, battery pack and spare headlamp
- Earphones
- **Miscellaneous**
  - Passport
  - Fickaskap Waterproof phone case, which also doubles as a wallet and passport holder
  - Bank cards (one in the wallet, one hidden in my frame bag)
  - Two velcro straps to attach things to the frame if necessary
  - Sunglasses
  - Spectacles
  - Cleat covers
  - One spare cleat and bolts
  - Wrist band with personal identity information
  - Tennis ball to massage my bum. (Not something I would have spontaneously taken, but a physiotherapist gave it to me at the last minute and it was surprisingly helpful)